Thriving Through The End Times

Dr. Neil T. Anderson

Published by Freedom In Christ Ministries International
4 Beacontree Plaza, Gillette Way, Reading RG2 0BS, UK.
www.freedominchrist.org

First edition 2023.

ISBN: 978-1-913082-64-2

Cover Design: Amber Weigand-Buckley, #barefacedcreativemedia

Contents

Foreword

By Steve Goss,
President
Freedom in Christ Ministries International

Since Dr. Anderson founded our discipleship ministry over thirty years ago, Freedom in Christ has equipped millions of Christians worldwide to cultivate a lifestyle of unstoppable spiritual growth.

Neil (as he prefers to be called) developed a Biblical approach to discipleship that still seems unique, and our vision is to equip the Church to bring transformation to every nation and generation. The goal is to make fruitful disciples who can reproduce themselves and impact their communities. As a result, we now have self-sustaining offices in over thirty countries (I invite you to read our core values in Appendix B).

Neil has written well over one hundred books that have been hugely appreciated by millions – perhaps tens of millions – of Christians. The message God has given him has been embraced right across the Church, by every major denomination by Evangelicals, Pentecostals, and Charismatics alike. It's used by discipleship, counseling, and addictive recovery ministries, as well as all kinds of small group ministries.

Thriving Through the End Times is Neil's "final reflection" upon his journey to the center of God's will and the dangers currently facing the Church.

He considers the very real possibility that we are facing the end times and a coming apostasy, and helps us understand where we are vulnerable to deception. Neil, like Paul, is "...afraid that, as the serpent deceived Eve by his craftiness, your minds will be led astray from the simplicity and purity of devotion to Christ" (2 Corinthians 11:3). He calls attention to Paul's clear warning in 1 Timothy 4:1 – "But the Spirit explicitly says that in later times some will fall away from the faith, paying attention to deceitful spirits and teachings of demons" – and shows how this is, in fact, happening right now.

Neil starts by looking at threats that affect us on a wider level and helps us understand how legalism, liberalism, spiritism, and elitism are major encumbrances that draw us away from the gospel of grace and Christ-centered living. I have heard him say on a number of occasions that heresy usually begins with the truth out of balance, and he puts his finger accurately on areas where we risk becoming dangerously unbalanced.

A health warning: it would be impossible for Neil to warn the Church about the dangers of moving too far in a particular direction without somebody feeling that he was stepping on their toes. If that happens to you, don't take it personally – you can rest assured that someone heading too far in the opposite direction is feeling the same thing! And please keep reading, because I would hate for you to miss the book's second half, where Neil brings it all down to a personal level.

You will be so encouraged as He helps you discern between good and evil, learn what it means to pray, live by the Spirit, and seek real intimacy with God.

Are we in the end times? We can't know for sure. But if we are, this book will help you not only survive but thrive as a fruitful disciple of Jesus.

Let us "…lay aside every encumbrance and the sin which so easily entangles us and let us run with endurance the race that is set before us…" (Hebrews 12:1).

Acknowledgment

I am not a self-made man. I wasn't even looking for God when He found me. I was an aerospace engineer when God called me into full-time ministry, which surprised me almost as much as it did my wife. I would have been content to be a pastor in a small country church. I was surprised again when I received the call to teach at Talbot School of Theology. I thought I had found my life's work in being a seminary professor and wasn't interested in looking elsewhere. I only founded Freedom in Christ Ministries to make material available. I never had any desire to write a book, but I was surprised again when two publishers sought me out. That led to my first two books, *Victory Over the Darkness* (Bethany House), and *The Bondage Breaker* (Harvest House), which have both sold over two million copies. Their success was why I left the seminary and incorporated Freedom in Christ Ministries.

Over the years I have never gone where I wasn't invited. I have never charged for the ministry I have rendered to individuals or put a price tag on my ministry. We have never advertised, but we now have offices and representatives in thirty countries. I can truly say that I am what I am by the grace of God.

This book is my final reflection on my own journey to the center of God's will. I want to thank my son, Karl, who took his mother's place as the first person to edit my work. And I want to thank Steve Goss for doing the final edit, and for providing excellent leadership over Freedom in Christ Ministries. Whatever is true and balanced in this book is to be credited to God's guidance over fifty years of ministry.

Neil T. Anderson

Introduction

But realize this, that in the last days, difficult times will come. For men will be lovers of self, lovers of money, boastful, arrogant, revilers, disobedient to parents, ungrateful, unholy, unloving, irreconcilable, malicious gossips, without self-control, brutal, haters of good, treacherous, reckless, conceited, lovers of pleasure rather than lovers of God, holding to a form of godliness, although they have denied its power; Avoid such men as these.

2 Timothy 3:1-5

I don't know if Paul had our present day in mind, but I do know that the entire world is facing "difficult times." What is now happening in the world is unprecedented in human history. Various locations of this fallen world have always had plagues, droughts, storms, and skirmishes between nations, but what we are experiencing today is global. International meetings are being held to discuss global climate change. World currencies are in a state of flux with national and personal debt escalating. The Coronavirus pandemic was global and so is the uncensored internet. Those who own a cell phone can be instantly apprised of every opinion and current event taking place in the world. Artificial intelligence is just that; artificial. Software is available that can alter images, making it appear that people are saying the opposite of what they believe. The possibility of being deceived by the media has never been greater. Those in power seek to control the narrative by censoring those who disagree with them. Free speech is under attack, and globalists are trying to unite the world ruled by whom? That is the ultimate question.

The era of postmodernism has rejected absolute truth thus marginalizing the Church, which is "the pillar and support of the truth" (1 Timothy 3:15). The liberal progressive movement espouses a godless form of Marxism seeking to cancel the Judeo-Christian culture that the United States and much of western civilization was founded on. Without the moral restraint of the Church, all forms of lawlessness prevail. Every form of sexual deviancy is acceptable, and you will be censored if you speak against them. Marriage is no longer a sacred union between a man and a woman, and not even considered honorable by some. Abortion has become a common means of birth control right up to the time of delivery. Big tech, liberal politicians, universities, and the press have aligned themselves against the Church, which is becoming an enemy of the State. "If the foundations are being destroyed what can the righteous do" (Psalm 11:3)?

In his article, *"The Decay of Greatness,"*[1] Ed Vitagliano cited several studies that concluded:

In the records of history ... there is no example of a society displaying great energy for any appreciable period unless it has been absolutely monogamous ... Since a disorderly sexual life tends to undermine the physical and mental health, morality, and creativity of its devotees, it has a similar effect upon a society that is composed largely of profligates. And the greater the number of profligates, and the more debauched their behavior, the graver the consequences for the whole society. And if sexual anarchists compose any considerable proportion of its membership, they eventually destroy the society itself.

The apostle Paul explains this moral decline in Romans 1:18-32:

For the wrath of God is revealed from heaven against all ungodliness and unrighteousness of men who suppress the truth in unrighteousness, because that which is known about God is evident within them; for God made it evident to them. For since the creation of the world His invisible attributes, His eternal power and divine nature, have been clearly seen, being understood through what has been made, so that they are without excuse. For even though they knew God, they did not honor Him as God or give thanks, but they became futile in their speculations, and their foolish heart was darkened. Professing to be wise, they became fools, and exchanged the glory of the incorruptible God for an image in the form of corruptible man and of birds and four-footed animals and crawling creatures.

Therefore, God gave them over in the lusts of their hearts to impurity, so that their bodies would be dishonored among them. For they exchanged the truth of God for a lie and worshiped and served the creature rather than the Creator, who is blessed forever. Amen.

For this reason, God gave them over to degrading passions; for their women exchanged the natural function for that which is unnatural, and in the same way also the men abandoned the natural function of the woman and burned in their desire toward one another, men with men committing indecent acts and receiving in their own persons the due penalty of their error.

And just as they did not see fit to acknowledge God any longer, God gave them over to a depraved mind, to do those things which are not proper, being filled with all unrighteousness, wickedness, greed, evil; full of envy, murder, strife, deceit, malice: they are gossips, slanderers, haters of God, insolent, arrogant, boastful, inventors of evil, disobedient to parents, without understanding, untrustworthy, unloving, unmerciful; and although they know the ordinances of God, that those who practice such things are worthy of death, they not only do the same but also give hearty approval to those who practice them.

Western civilization is in the final stage of a "depraved (*adokimos*) mind," or reprobate mind. It means to fail the test, i.e., be unapproved. God cannot approve such a mind set and therefore must be rejected. Such depravity is the ultimate test for humanity. "Test yourselves to see if you are in the faith; examine yourselves! Or do you not recognize this about yourselves that Jesus Christ is in you – unless indeed *you fail the test* [*adokimos*, emphasis added]? But I trust that you will realize that we ourselves do not *fail the test* [*adokimos*, emphasis added]" (2 Corinthians 13:5,6). Nothing can be clearer about our standing with God. "He who has the Son has the life; he who does not have the Son of God does not have the life" (1 John 5:12). Those who don't have the Son, "walk in the futility of their minds, being darkened in their understanding, excluded from the life of God because of the ignorance that is in them, because of the hardness of their heart" (Ephesians 4:17,18).

This descent into darkness is truly sad, because true believers should be like God who "desires all men to be saved and to come to the knowledge of the truth" (1 Timothy 2:4). "For I have no pleasure in the death of anyone who dies," declares the Lord God. "Therefore, repent and live" (Ezekiel 18:32). I have always tried to do the work of an evangelist and be a good witness, but my calling has led me to equip the Church. The purpose of Freedom in Christ Ministries is to equip churches worldwide enabling them to establish their people, marriages, and ministries to be alive and free in Christ through genuine repentance and faith in God to His honor and glory. As much as I am concerned for the lost, I am even more concerned for Christians and churches that are being tempted to compromise their faith. We have been clearly warned that there will be a falling away before the return of Christ (see 2 Thessalonians 2:1-4).

The pressure to fall away has never been greater. Spiritual forces are aligned against the Church and the family, and the latter is where we are most vulnerable. Jesus said (Matthew 10:34-36):

> Do not think that I came to bring peace on earth; I did not come to bring peace, but a sword. For I came to set a man against his father, and a daughter against her mother, and a daughter-in-law against her mother-in-law; and a man's enemies will be members of the household. He who loves father or mother more than me is not worthy of me; and he who loves son or daughter more than me is not worthy of me.

Jesus came to bring peace between the believer and Himself, but the inevitable result of Christ's first coming is conflict between Himself and the antichrist, between His children and the devil's children. That conflict can occur between members of the same household, which is why we are not to be unevenly yoked together. I know several individual believers who have stayed faithful to God without compromising their convictions and eventually saw their unbelieving spouses come to faith, but I have never met anyone who, by compromising their moral convictions, saw their spouse's conversion. Unbelievers don't respect people of faith when they don't live according to what they profess.

Just as concerning are those parents who change what they believe because family members announce they have adopted a lifestyle based on a false belief. That is loving a family member more than God, and doing so will not win them to Christ. Such prodigals need us to stand firm in our faith and be ready to welcome them home when the consequences of their choices catch up with them.

A local church sponsored an evangelist whom they commissioned to plant a church. Being a gifted communicator, the church grew to 1,200 attendees within a couple of years. They called together a committee to tackle the question of same-sex marriage and other progressive challenges. The pastor told a local reporter that they decided to approach the topic from a sociological perspective rather than a theological perspective, which is absolutely nonsensical from an orthodox perspective. They adopted same-sex marriages and other progressive agendas. The result is predictable. They went from 1200 to 150 within six months, and the pastor resigned to share his "insights" with other pastors. A mutual friend tried to reason with him but concluded that he was not redeemable.

How can we prevent such apostasy, and how then should we live in these end times? To ask the question brings to mind the oft-viewed cartoon caricature of a monk holding a sign saying, "Repent, for the end is near." But that is exactly what we need to do. "For it is time for judgment, to begin with the household of God" (1 Peter 4:17). Jesus told us to take the log out of our own eyes so that we will be able to clearly see the speck in our brother's eye. Let's not be caught cursing the darkness when we should be turning on the light. All the darkness of the world cannot extinguish the light of one candle.

Conspiracy theories abound in such times as these, but our faith rests upon what we know to be true, not on speculations about the future. The conflict between the Kingdom of God and the kingdom of darkness is being waged right now. Who are the players and who is pulling the strings? Who are the rulers of this world? To answer those questions requires a Christ-centered biblical worldview that takes into account the reality of the spiritual world.

In Chapter One, I will explain what I believe is a balanced perspective of the natural world and the spiritual realm in which we live. The goal is to see this world from God's perspective and strengthen the foundation upon which we lay our faith.

In Chapters Two through Six, I will explain how to overcome legalism, liberalism, false prophets, and teachers, spiritism, and Satanism. All five are enemies of the gospel, and all five are embedded in various churches and denominations. Therefore, let us "...lay as de every encumbrance and the sin which so easily entangles us, and let us run with endurance the race that is set before us, fixing our eyes on Jesus, the author and perfecter of faith..." (Hebrews 12:1,2).

It is not enough to resolve personal and spiritual conflicts through genuine repentance and faith in God. If that is all we, did it would be like a ship that has thrown off all the mooring lines. The ship is free, but it will be tossed and turned by the sea. To navigate our way through troubled times we have to be empowered and guided by the Holy Spirit. To do this we must have our senses trained to discern good and evil and learn what it means to pray and live by the Spirit, which are the subjects of Chapters Seven through Nine. All this requires an intimate relationship with God, which I will explain in Chapter Ten.

Jesus said, "When the Son of Man comes, will He find faith on the earth?" (Luke 18:8). If we are approaching end times, the only pertinent question is, "What sort of people ought you to be in holy conduct and godliness?" (2 Peter 3:11). The fundamental question is not what we should do, but who we should be. Nobody can keep us from being the person God created us to be, and that is God's will for our lives. What it takes to stop us is the test of our character. "Many false prophets will arise and will mislead many. Because lawlessness is increased, most people's love will grow cold, but the one who endures to the end, he will be saved" (Matthew 24:11:13).

Neil T. Anderson

Chapter One: Toward A Biblical Worldview

Why does He call the devil the ruler of this world? Because virtually the whole of humanity surrendered to him. All are his voluntary and willing slaves. Few pay any heed to Christ, who promises unnumbered blessings. They follow the devil, who promises nothing but leads them all to hell. He rules in this age, where he has... more subjects than God, more who obey him rather than God. All but a few are in his grasp on account of their laxity.[2]

Chrysostom, Homily on Ephesians

"In the beginning, God created the heavens and the earth" (Genesis 1:1). We know about the earth, but what are the heavens? To answer that question, let's begin with what we can observe and what we know from recorded history. I was an electrical engineer when the Hubble Telescope was developed, which allowed us to view the extravagance of creation as never before. On December 25, 2021, the James Webb Space Telescope was launched, which is many times more powerful than the Hubble Telescope. What we can now see is beyond our ability to comprehend. There are supernovas, mysterious black holes, and multitudes of other galaxies much larger than our own. "The heavens are telling of the glory of God; and their expanse is declaring the work of His hand" (Psalm 19:1). All this created matter is finite, devoid of life, and did not originate from preexisting matter. On the other hand, the Creator is living, infinite, the mind behind the universe.

The earth has organic life in the form of plants, birds, animals, and fish. Such life is subject to the natural law of death. It perpetuates its species by sowing seeds or bearing young for the next generation before it dies; otherwise, the species would become extinct. With all that in place, "The Lord God formed man of dust from the ground and breathed into his nostrils the breath of life; and man became a living being" (Genesis 2:7). Something new and different was introduced into the universe. God shared His divine and eternal life with Adam, who was created in His image and likeness. His soul was in union with God. He could have lived forever if he had eaten only from the tree of life. He was warned that if he ate from the tree of the knowledge of good and evil, he would surely die but Eve was deceived by Satan, and Adam made the fatal choice to eat the forbidden fruit and died spiritually. Their souls were no longer in union with God (i.e., they were spiritually dead), but their souls were still in union with their bodies (i.e., they were physically alive). Adam remained physically alive for 930 years. All their descendants would be subject to the law of sin and death because they are all born physically alive, but spiritually dead (see Ephesians 2:1). They also surrendered their dominion over planet earth, and Satan became the ruler of this world.

To overcome the fall of humanity, God had to accomplish three primary objectives. First, He sent His Son to die for our sins, thus removing the barriers between Him and us. Second, Jesus was resurrected in order that we may have eternal life in Christ. What Adam and Eve lost in the fall was life, i.e., union with God, and that is what Jesus came to give us. Third, "The Son of God appeared for this purpose, to destroy the works of the devil" (1 John 3:8). Notice in Colossians 2:13-15 that all three objectives were accomplished:

> When you were dead in your transgressions and the uncircumcision of your flesh, He made you alive together with Him, having forgiven us all our transgressions, having canceled out the certificate of debt consisting of decrees against us, which was hostile to us; and He has taken it out of the way, having nailed it to the cross. When He had disarmed the rulers and authorities, He made a public display of them, having triumphed over them through Him.

The Unseen Realm

Most believers have some understanding of the gospel, and how history has unfolded on planet earth, but little awareness of the spiritual realm that surrounds them. Before the creation of Adam and Eve, God created His original family, referred to in Scripture as the sons of God. They make up the host of heaven, and our Heavenly Father is the LORD of hosts (Psalm 24:10). Both GOD and the sons of God are identified by the Hebrew word, "*Elohim*," which is also the most common name for GOD, our Heavenly Father, in the Old Testament. *Elohim* has been variously translated as 'God,' 'gods,' 'rulers,' and 'heavenly beings.' Context defines meaning. For instance, "God (*Elohim*) takes His stand in His own congregation; He judges in the midst of the rulers (*Elohim*)" (Psalm 82:1). GOD is saying to the host of heaven, "You are gods, and all of you are sons of the Most High" (vs. 6).[3] Obviously they are corruptible since a third fell from heaven, and they, "will die like men and fall like any one of the princes" (vs. 7). This is not Pantheism. There is only one true Trinitarian GOD (*Yahweh*, Jehovah) who is the Creator and the ultimate authority in the universe.

Our natural senses cannot see the spiritual realm, but we can see its effects everywhere. Scripture, however, occasionally pulls back the curtain and gives us a glimpse of what is happening in the spiritual realm. When the king of Aram was warring against Israel, Elisha was divulging all his plans to the king of Israel. So, the king of Aram sent his army to destroy him. "Now when the attendant of the man of God had risen early and gone out, behold an army of horses and chariots was circling the city. And his servant said to him, 'Alas, my master! What shall we do?' So, he answered, 'Do not fear, for those who are with us are more than those who are with them.' Then Elisha prayed and said, 'O LORD, I pray, open his eyes that he may see.' And the LORD opened the servant's eyes and he saw, and behold, the mountain was full of horses and chariots of fire all around Elisha" (2 Kings 6:15-17). When the army advanced toward Elisha, he prayed and asked God to strike them with blindness, which He did, and they were led away to Samaria. Believers today should know that, "Greater is He who is in you than he who is in the world" (1 John 4:4).

On another occasion, the king of Israel was soliciting the help of Jehoshaphat, the king of Judah, who requested that they first inquire of the LORD. So, the king of Israel gathered his false prophets who told him what he wanted to hear, but Jehoshaphat knew they weren't telling the truth. So, they called for a true prophet named Micaiah who told the king of Israel the truth, which he didn't want to hear, and gave them a vision of heaven in 1 Kings 22:19-22:

> Micaiah said, "Hear the word of the Lord, I saw the LORD sitting on His throne, and all the hosts of heaven standing by Him on His right and on His left. The LORD said, "Who will entice Ahab to go up to Ramoth-Gilead?" And one said this while another said that. Then a spirit came forward and stood before the LORD and sa d, 'I will entice him.' The LORD said to him, 'how?' And he sa d, 'I will go out and be a deceiving spirit in the mouth of all his prophets., Then He said, 'You are to entice him and also to prevail, Go and do so.'"

At some time before the advent of Adam and Eve, Satan led a rebellion against GOD resulting in a third of the heavenly host [*Elohim*] being expelled. In the New Testament, they are called evil spirits or demons. When Adam sinned and lost dominion, Satan became the ruler of this world (John 16:11) overseeing a hierarchy of demons. True prophets receive their message from GOD, but they are vastly outnumbered by false prophets who are governed by the ruler of this world. For instance, Elijah stood alone against 400 false prophets (see 1 Kings 22:6).

Spiritual warfare and redemption are the dominant themes of the Bible, depicting a battle between good and evil, between false prophets and true prophets, between the father of lies and the Spirit of truth, between the anti-Christ and Christ, and we are in that battle whether we like or believe it, or not. The good news is, "He rescued us from the domain of darkness, and transferred us to the kingdom of His beloved Son, in whom we have redemption, the forgiveness of sins" (Colossians 1:13,14). All that we have and can hope for is based on our identity and position in Christ as children of God. "As many as received Him, to them He gave the right to become children of God" (John 1:12).

Heaven and Heavenlies

Throughout Church history, the word "heaven" has been depicted in three different ways. First, heaven is the abode of God as referenced in the Lord's Prayer, "Our Father who art in Heaven." Second, there are the stellar heavens pertaining to the stars as used in Psalm 19:1, "The heavens and the earth are declaring and showing forth the glory of God." Finally, there is the atmospheric heaven or heavenlies, which is the spiritual realm surrounding the earth. It is in this realm that we exist and are spiritually blessed (Ephesians 1:3). The spiritual realm is not some far-off place. It engulfs the atmosphere around us, just as radio waves do, which are also undetectable by our natural senses.

Paul uses the term "heavenly places" ("heavenly realms" in the NIV) five times in the book of Ephesians. Christ's triumph over sin and death resulted in Him being seated "at His (God's) right hand in the heavenly places, far above all rule and authority and power and dominion, and every name that is named, not only in this age but also in the one to come" (Ephesians 1:20-21).

"But God being rich in mercy, because of His great love with which He loved us, even when we were dead in our transgressions, made us alive together with Christ (by grace you have been saved), and raised us with Him in the heavenly places in Christ Jesus" (Ephesians 2:4-6). Those who have been made alive in Christ share in Christ's exaltation and enthronement in the heavenly places. This was necessary, "so that the manifold wisdom of God might now be made known through the church to the rulers and the authorities in the heavenly places. This was in accordance with the eternal purpose which He carried out in Christ Jesus our Lord, in whom we have boldness and confident access through faith in Him" (Ephesians 3:10-12). To summarize: it is the eternal purpose of God to make His wisdom known through the Church (all true believers) to the rulers and authorities in the spiritual realm. Satan doesn't perfectly know the future, although false prophets and modern-day psychics will try to predict it. God's future plans will be made known to the demonic hierarchy through the Church.

Consequently, "Our struggle is not against flesh and blood, but against the rulers, against the powers, against the world forces of this darkness, against the spiritual forces of wickedness in the heavenly places" (Ephesians 6:12). The struggle is not something that takes place in the future. A war against God and His saints is happening now.

Most evangelical seminaries in the West have taught that Paul was writing to correct the false teaching of Gnosticism. It is now known, however, that Gnosticism didn't threaten the Church until the middle of the second century. The real threat to the early Church was occultism and the worship of false gods. The best I have read on this subject is Dr. Clinton Arnold's book, *Powers of Darkness*,[4] subtitled *"Principalities and Powers in Paul's Letters."*

Gaining Focus and Balance

A biblical worldview must take into account two realms, heaven, and earth. In other words, there is a spiritual realm and a natural realm, and there are two types of players: humans and spiritual beings (*Elohim*). To see the role angels play, see Appendix A. A mature believer is aware of both and has learned how to live in both realms at the same time. To understand how we do that, consider the following diagram:

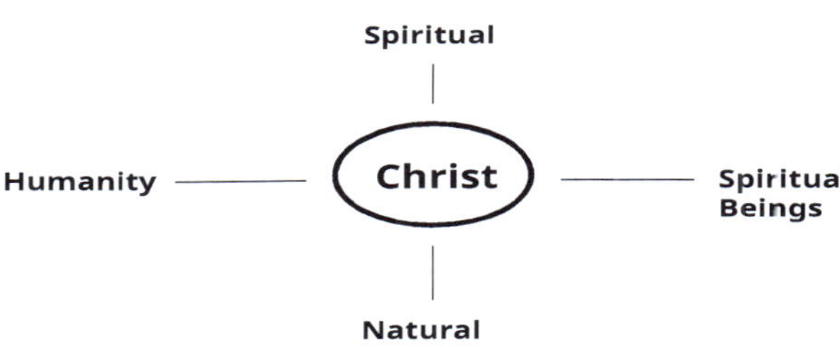

Keep in mind that I am not pitting opposites against each other, but rather illustrating the need for a focused and balanced understanding of reality. If you put more emphasis on the spiritual realm you move up on the diagram. If you put more emphasis on the role humans play, you move to the left on the diagram. If all you see is humanity and a natural world you are in the far left and lower corner and far from Christ. If you put more emphasis on the role that spiritual beings play, you move to the right, etc.

Christ is the center of the diagram because He was fully God and fully man, and He lived a perfectly balanced life in both the natural and the spiritual realms, leaving us an example to follow in His steps. History recorded in the Gospels reveals that Jesus had complete authority and power over the natural as well as the spiritual realm. Consequently, Jesus precisely knew the activity of deceiving spirits and how they influence humanity, and He knows what is on the hearts of those who are being deceived. Even His chosen disciples were vulnerable. After Peter made a divinely enlightened profession of faith that Jesus is the Christ, Peter rebuked Jesus for saying He was going to be crucified. But Jesus knew where that thought was coming from, and said, "Get behind Me, Satan! You are a stumbling block to Me, for you are not setting your mind on God's interests, but man's" (Matthew 16:23). On another occasion Jesus said, "Simon, Simon, behold, Satan has demanded permission to sift you like wheat" (Luke 22:31). The disciples had been arguing as to which of them was regarded to be the greatest (vs. 24), and such pride resulted in Peter denying Jesus three times. To stay focused we have to fix our eyes on Jesus, the author and perfecter of our faith (Hebrews 12:2).

A western worldview is skewed to the lower half of the diagram. The secular education I received was based on rationalism (everything can be understood through reason) and naturalism (all that exists can be observed through our natural senses). In my youth I faithfully attended church, but I thought eternal life was something I would receive when I died and went to heaven, wherever that was! It was like living in a one-story house where only our natural senses come into play. All I knew was contained inside those walls, and the spiritual world was in the attic where we never ventured. In reality, there is no attic. All natural and spiritual activities are happening on the first floor, which has no ceilings or walls. There was a whole universe of reality that lay behind my experience and exposure. There are no natural barriers for the spiritual world. It was hard for me, and it is for most westerners, to embrace the reality of the spiritual world, which according to Paul is just as real as the natural world, and maybe more so. "While we look not at the things which are seen, but at the things which are not seen; for the things which are seen are temporal, but the things which are not seen are eternal" (2 Corinthians 4:18).

Reality Check

The present world we are living in is co-habited by humanity, a hierarchy of demons ruled by Satan, and our omnipresent Heavenly Father along with angelic beings. "The serpent of old who is called the devil and Satan, *who deceives the whole world*; he was thrown down to the earth, and his angels were thrown down with him (Revelation 12:9, emphasis added). "We know that we are of God, and that *the whole world lies in the power of the evil one*" (1 John 5:19, emphasis added). Finally, "The Spirit clearly says that in later times some will abandon the faith and follow deceiving spirits and things taught by demons" (1 Timothy 4:1). I can personally attest to the fact that this is happening right now all over the world.

Most believers understand Satan to be the tempter and accuser of the brethren who accuses us before God, day and night (see Revelation 12:10). Who hasn't struggled with tempting and condemning thoughts? You will likely know when you are being tempted and accused, but when you are deceived, you don't know it. We don't overcome deception by human reasoning or research, but rather by divine revelation. That is why Jesus prayed, "I do not ask You to take them out of the world, but to keep them from the evil one. They are not of the world, even as I am not of the world. Sanctify them in the truth; Your word is truth" (John 17:15-17). You win the battle for your mind when you "let the word of Christ richly dwell within you" (Colossians 3:16).

How are we going to "...make disciples of all the nations..." (Matthew 28:19), if "the god of this world has blinded the minds of the unbelieving" (2 Corinthians 4:4)? It is impossible to accomplish all that God has planned for the Church unless we have a biblical worldview. Those who don't are like blindfolded warriors striking out at themselves and each other.

Mystery Revealed

In Ephesians 2:1-3 the apostle Paul describes the condition of non-believers before they came to Christ. "And you were dead (spiritually) in your trespasses and sins, in which you formerly walked according to the course of this world, according to *the prince of the power of the air* (emphasis added, literally: "ruler [*archon*] of the authority of the air"), of the spirit that is now working in the sons of disobedience, among them we too all formerly lived in the lusts of our flesh, indulging the desires of the flesh and of the mind, and were by nature children of wrath, even as the rest." In other words, unbelievers are in the kingdom of darkness governed by Satan. Jesus said the ruler (*archon*) of this world would be cast out (John 12:31) and has already been judged (16:11) So, when Jesus proclaimed that the kingdom of God was at hand, Satan had to do what he could to stop it or be dethroned as the ruler of this world. In doing so he unwittingly played right into God's hand as explained in 1 Corinthians 2:6-8:

> Yet we do speak wisdom among those who are mature; a wisdom, however, not of this age nor of the rulers (*archonites*) of this age who are passing away; but we speak God's wisdom which God predestined before the ages to our glory; the wisdom which none of the rulers (*archonites*) of this age has understood; for if they had understood it they would not have crucified the Lord of glory.

Lacking a biblical worldview, you might think that the rulers were Jewish officials who were destined to die physically, but that is not what the passage is saying. "Rulers" (*archonites*) are spiritual beings. "Passing away" (*katargeo*) means destroyed or abolished as in 1 Corinthians 15:24-26, "then comes the end, when He hands over the kingdom to the God and Father, when He has abolished (*katargeo*) all rule and all authority and power. For He must reign until He has put all His enemies under His feet. The last enemy that will be abolished is death." That was achieved with the resurrection.

Mystery does not mean mysterious, but rather a truth that has not yet been fully revealed. Satan is the ruler (*archon*) of this world facing an impending doom along with his demonic rulers (*archonites*) who are now working in the "sons of disobedience," i.e.. those who are "born dead in their trespasses and sins." Satan knew nothing of the coming resurrection and neither did Jesus's disciples, and not even the angels. Satan thought he could prevent the coming of God's kingdom by crucifying Christ, which was a fatal mistake. If Satan had known that Jesus would be resurrected, he would not have "crucified the Lord of glory." Ambrose[5], one of the four doctors of the western church, wrote in the late fourth century:[6]

> "The Jewish rulers cannot be called rulers of this age because they were subject to the Romans. Nor did the Romans crucify Jesus, because Pilate himself said that he found no fault in him. The rulers who crucified Him were the demons. They knew that Jesus was the Messiah but not that He was the Son of God, and so it can be said they crucified Him in ignorance."

Did the high priest, scribes, and Pharisees know they were being led by Satan when they sought to crucify Jesus? I don't think so, but Jesus affirmed that they were. He wasn't speaking with hyperbole when He said to them, "You are of your father the devil, and you want to do the desires of your father. He was a murderer from the beginning and does not stand in the truth because there is no truth in him. Whenever he speaks a lie, he speaks from his own nature, for he is a liar and the father of lies" (John 8:44). Satan had so deceived the Jewish hierarchy that Jesus had little choice but to choose His disciples from the working class and conduct most of His ministry outside of Jerusalem.

Did Peter know that he was a spokesperson for Satan when Jesus rebuked him? No. Did David know he was being deceived, "when Satan stood up against Israel and moved David to number Israel" (1 Chronicles 21:1)? I don't think he did, but Joab knew it was sinful and warned him against it. David did it anyway and thousands died, because of his sin. Those were David's thoughts, or at least he thought they were, and therein lies the deception. Did Judas know that Satan had entered him (see Luke 22:3) and that Satan had put into his heart to betray Jesus (see John 13:2)? I doubt it. With no knowledge of the coming resurrection, Judas probably thought he was forcing the Lord's hand to inaugurate the kingdom that would overthrow Rome. The fact that he was a thief probably made him vulnerable. He hung himself when he realized what he had done.

Did Ananias and Sapphira know that Satan had filled their hearts to lie to the Holy Spirit (see Acts 5:3)? Again, I doubt it. The word "filled" is the same word encouraging us to be "...filled with the Spirit" (Ephesians 5:18) and means to be controlled. Some would like to dismiss them as unbelievers, but New Testament scholar F.F. Bruce argued that Ananias was a believer,[7] and Ernest Haenchen wrote that he (Ananias) was a Jewish Christian and commented, "Satan has filled his heart. Ananias has lied to the Holy Spirit inasmuch as the Spirit is present in Peter (and in the community). Hence, in the last resort, it is not simply two men who confront one another but in them the Holy Spirit and Satan, whose instruments they are."[8]

The high priest, scribes, and Pharisees were "Jerusalem insiders," not unlike the "Washington insiders" of our present day, who seek to retain their authority and power by lies and deceit if necessary. Most are totally unaware that they are being deceived by the father of lies. There are some, however, who actually worship Satan, and are fully aware of whom they serve (see chapter six).

Ignorance and Arrogance

Only the biblically illiterate, the intellectually arrogant, or the uninformed deny the reality of the spiritual world. Jesus said we need to "...become like children to enter the kingdom of God..." (Matthew 18:3). When Jesus sent the twelve disciples out to proclaim the kingdom of God, He gave them power and authority over all the demons (Luke 9:1). Then Jesus appointed 70 others and they returned "with joy saying, 'even the demons are subject to us in Your name'" (Luke 10:17). This prompted Jesus to pray, "I praise You, O Father, LORD of heaven and earth, that You have hidden these things from the wise and intelligent and have revealed them to infants" (Luke 10:21). We have a choice to humble ourselves or be humbled, because pride will keep us from having an intimate relationship with God.

Have you ever met someone who is spiritually arrogant? They have been spiritually "enlightened" and can see and know things others don't. Have you ever met those who are theologically arrogant, and anybody who disagrees with them is wrong? Or perhaps you have known arrogant natural or social scientists who think they have life figured out and dismiss the uneducated or religious? Maybe you know of some arrogant elitists who think they are superior to the common person. Notice in the following diagram that those furthest from Christ in either direction is marked by ignorance or arrogance:

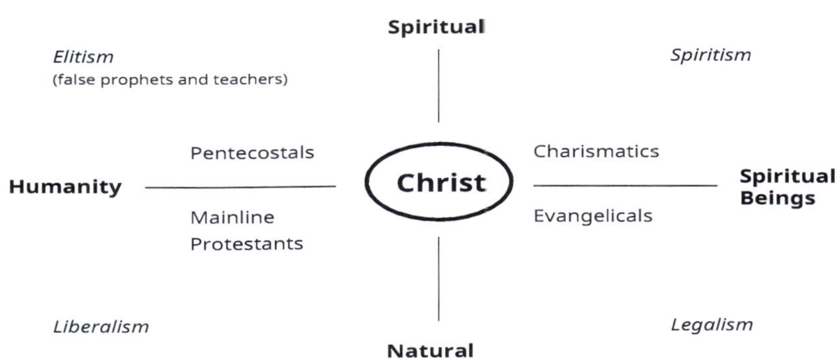

Those furthest from Christ are in league with the father of lies, who was cast from Heaven because of pride and rebellion. Such sins of the spirit are not as obvious as the sins of the flesh but are much more deadly. Humility is the mark of a mature believer, not prideful arrogance.

Evangelicalism is a western orientation that grew out of fundamentalism. The danger to those in this quadrant is that they lapse into legalism, which is a major encumbrance to running the race set before us. We are "servants of a new covenant, not of the letter, but of the Spirit; for the letter kills, but the Spirit gives life" (2 Corinthians 3:6). I will address the bondage to legalism in Chapter Two.

The older mainline denominations have progressively become more liberal. The worldview depicted in the lower left quadrant focuses more on the natural world and the role humans play. Sociology, psychology, psychiatry, and most of our medical models have this worldview. Those furthest from Christ pay little attention to God, even less to the god of this world, and arrogantly dismiss those who profess otherwise. If you grew up in that culture, you are likely to be ignorant of the spiritual world. Fortunately, there are some humble and godly doctors and psychologists. I will deal with liberalism/humanism in Chapter Three.

Over the years I have been invited to speak in many denominations, half of which would be considered Pentecostal or Charismatic. Both tend to give more emphasis to the spiritual realm. In recent years the most impressive growth of the Church has been in the southern hemisphere, and it is largely Pentecostal. I suspect that is partly due to their emphasis on the spiritual world which is more relatable to countries steeped in spiritism. The danger in this quadrant is to elevate the stature of elite leaders promising healing and prosperity. Followers will attend massive meetings hoping their lives will be changed for the better because of the presence of some anointed person. If you are looking for a man to save you, He has already come. In Chapter Four I will address the problem of false teachers, prophets and messiahs that will be present in end times.

Charismatics tend to rely more on the Holy Spirit rather than some anointed person, and they emphasize the gifts of the Spirit more than evangelical churches tend to. The danger here is to lack discernment and fall sway to spiritism, unwittingly paying attention to deceiving spirits.

It is terribly unfortunate that we identify ourselves as Protestants, evangelicals, Pentecostals, or charismatics. Those are man-made divisions in the Church and so are the 20,000 different denominations. Jesus prayed that we would all be one, and we can only be one in Christ. Paul wrote, "I implore you to walk in a manner worthy of the calling with which you have been called, with all humility and gentleness, with patience, showing tolerance for one another in love, being diligent to preserve the unity of the Spirit in the bond of peace. There is one body and one Spirit, just as also you were called in one hope of your calling: one Lord, one faith, one baptism, one God and Father of all who is over all and through all and in all" (Ephesians 4:1-6). A heretic is one who causes divisions, and heresy often begins with truth out of balance. Divisions happen when we major in the minors.

Satan's strategy is to cause divisions. First, he will try to divide your mind, because a double-minded man is unstable in all his ways (James 1:8). Then he will try to divide those who have become one in Christ through marriage, because a house divided against itself cannot stand, and neither will a society. Finally, he will try to divide the Church, because united we stand, but divided we fall. We lose our impact when we present ourselves as a fragmented body, but a united Church is salt and light to a tasteless and dark world.

Conservative missiologists agree that the dominant religious orientation of the world is spiritism and has been since Satan became the ruler of this world. There are more practicing spiritists in the world than there are members in any one organized religion. You don't need to convince them that there is a spiritual world. They make sacrifices to appease the deities, and consult their mediums, quack doctors, and witch doctors to ward off evil spirits using incantations or spells to manipulate the spiritual world for protection, healing, or personal gain. Jesus came to undo the works of Satan and those who are alive in Christ have authority over demons. That is the gospel they are waiting to hear, and it is just as essential as forgiveness of sins and new life in Christ.

Don't think for a minute that Satan isn't just as active in North America and Europe. For instance, France has more psychic healers than medical doctors. More people in the United States read their daily horoscopes than have devotions in the Bible. Late night television has a parade of psychics offering guidance and prosperity. Such ads have recently crept into prime time, and for a dollar a minute you can consult a psychic in California. I will deal with spiritism in Chapter Five.

When it comes to helping others, each quadrant has a different emphasis as follows:

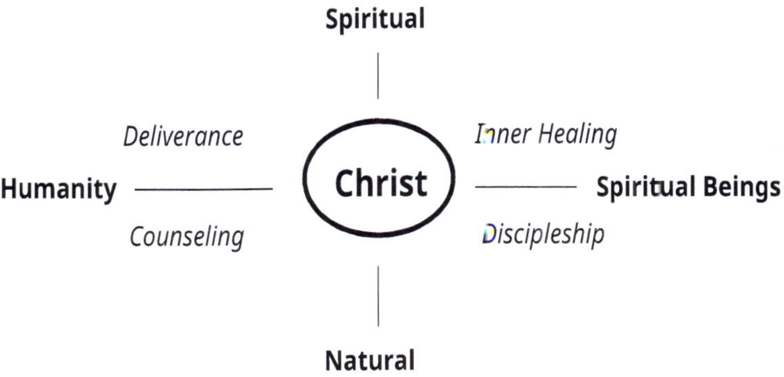

Please understand that I have been making broad generalizations about each quadrant. Any one church could be doing all four ministries, but unless they are perfectly balanced, they will place a greater emphasis on one over the others. Our staff and associates around the world have come from all four worldviews, but hopefully, they are all seeking to become more Christ-centered and balanced in their understanding of the world we live in. I was raised in a liberal church. When I found Christ, I became a mainstream evangelical and focused on discipleship. Continuing education and experience have moved me closer to Christ, and much more aware of the spiritual world. In the next four chapters, I will show how we accomplish inner healing, and deliverance through a process called discipleship counseling. Unless we help our people overcome their personal and spiritual conflicts, they are likely to become disillusioned with Christianity and fall away. It is my firm conviction that repentance and faith in God are the only means by which that can be accomplished. Jesus said, "The time is fulfilled, and the kingdom of God is at hand; repent and believe the gospel" (Mark 1:15).

Discussion Questions

1. What are the three essential elements of the gospel?
2. Who are the hosts of heaven?
3. *Elohim* is the most common name for God in the Old Testament. What differentiates *Yahweh* from another *Elohim*?
4. What conclusions can be drawn from the vision in 1 Kings 22:19-22 about *God* and how He governs, and the impact of the spiritual world?
5. Why should spiritual warfare be considered a dominant theme of the Bible?
6. If you go to heaven, where are you going? Is it a physical location or another dimension?
7. What does it mean to be seated with Christ in the heavenly places? What is our purpose for being there?
8. How are we supposed to live in the natural world and in the spiritual realm at the same time? Which do you think has the greater impact on how we live?
9. Explain the mystery that was revealed in 1 Corinthians 2:6-8. How are the Jerusalem "insiders" any different from the Washington "insiders" and other elitists in the world?
10. Most believers think they are living a balanced life, but they are evaluating that based on their own worldview, and they will evaluate others from their perspective. How would you explain your present worldview? How can you gain a more biblical worldview, and why should every believer be more open-minded and desirous of that?

Chapter Two:
Overcoming Legalism

For as many as are of the works of the Law are under a curse; for it is written, Cursed is everyone who does not abide by all things written in the book of the Law, to perform them [Deuteronomy 27:26]. Now that no one is justified by the Law before God, is evident; for the righteous man shall live by faith [Habakkuk 2:4]. However, the Law is not of faith; on the contrary, He who practices them shall live by them [Leviticus 18:5]. Christ redeemed us from the curse of the Law, having become a curse for us - for it is written, Cursed is everyone who hangs on a tree [Deuteronomy 21:23] - in order that in Christ Jesus the blessing of Abraham might come to the Gentiles so that we would receive the promise of the Spirit through faith.

Galatians 3:10-14

It would not be right that the grace of the Spirit should come to one who was graceless or full of offense. We're blessed first by the taking away of the curse. Then, justified by faith, we receive the grace of the Holy Spirit. So, the cross has dissolved the curse, faith has brought righteousness, and by God's own righteousness, the grace of the Spirit has been given.[9]

Chrysostom, Homily on Galatians 3:14

In making a case for justification by faith in the passage above, Paul quoted four verses from the Old Testament. What was a shadow in the Old Testament is now revealed in the New Testament. We have received the promise of the Spirit, which we appropriate by faith. If it is evident to all believers that no one is justified by the Law, then the problem of legalism should be non-existent, but that is not the case.

If there is no condemnation for those who are in Christ Jesus (see Romans 8:1), then why do so many believers still feel condemned? To gain a better understanding we asked the George Barna Research Group to conduct research on Christian beliefs. Believers were asked to respond to statements that relate to legalism, which we reported in our book *Grace That Breaks the Chains*.[10] How would you respond to the following statements? First, "The Christian life is well summed-up as: trying hard to do what God commands." The result: 57% strongly agreed and 25% somewhat agreed. Second, "I feel like I don't measure up to God's expectations of me." The result: 58%

agreed (28% strongly, 30% somewhat). We intentionally chose words in the next statement that Christians normally shy away from like rigid and strict. Third, "Rigid rules and strict standards are an important part of the life and teaching of my church." The result: 39% strongly agreed and 27% somewhat agreed. Apparently, many of God's children still feel like they are living under the curse of The Law.

Under the Old Covenant based on the Law of Moses the high priest would enter the Holy of Holies once a year to make atonement for all the sins of Israel. He would undergo elaborate purification rites before he entered. It was considered a frightening experience to come before the presence of a holy God without doing so. The high priests attached bells to the hem of their garments, and a rope was tied to their legs. The other priests would listen for the bells as they waited outside the veil. If they didn't hear the bells the rope was there to pull him out. Now consider the vision given in Zechariah 3:1-5:

> Then he showed me Joshua the high priest standing before the angel of the Lord, and Satan standing at his right hand to accuse him. The Lord said to Satan, "The Lord rebuke you, Satan! Indeed, the Lord who has chosen Jerusalem rebuke you! Is this not a brand plucked from the fire?" Now Joshua was clothed with filthy garments and standing before the angel. He spoke and said to those who were standing before him, saying, "Remove the filthy garments from him." Again, he said to him, "See, I have taken your iniquity away from you and will clothe you with festal robes."

In the court of heaven, the Lord is the Judge. Satan is the prosecuting attorney who accuses the brethren "...before our God day and night" (Revelation 12:10). We are the accused standing before the Judge in filthy garments indicating that we have all sinned and fallen short of the glory of God. Jesus is our defense attorney. He is saying to the Judge; "Look at my hands, my side, and my feet. I died once for all their sins. I rest my case." Weighing the evidence, the Judge, pointing His finger at Satan, says, "The Lord rebuke you, Satan. These are my children snatched from the flames of hell, and they are now clothed in the righteousness of my beloved Son. Not guilty!"

Every struggling believer that I have had the privilege to help had one thing in common. None of them knew who they were in Christ and didn't understand what it meant to be a child of God. If the Holy Spirit is bearing witness with our spirit that we are children of God (see Romans 8:16), why are so many not sensing that? Additionally, many of these same people struggle with condemning, accusing, and blasphemous thoughts.

A gifted seminary student won the homiletics award for being the outstanding senior preacher, maintained an excellent grade point average, and was known as mister personality. He seemed destined for a successful ministry, but he committed adultery and limped away. He later attended my conference and wrote me the following letter:

> I've always figured I was a rotten, no good, dirty, stinking sinner, saved by grace yet failing God miserably every day. All I could look forward to was a lifetime of apologizing every night for not being the man I know God wants me to be, "... but I will try harder, Lord." As a firstborn, trying so hard to earn the approval of highly expectant parents, I've related to God the same way. He just couldn't possibly love me as much as He does other "better" believers. Oh sure. I'm saved by grace through faith, but really, I'm just hanging on until He gets tired of putting up with me here and brings me home to finally stop the failure in progress. Whew, what a treadmill.

> Neil, when you said, 'You're not a sinner, you're a saint,' in reference to our new identity in Christ, you totally blew me away! Isn't it strange that a guy could go clear through a good seminary, and never really latch on to the truth that he is indeed a new creation in Christ? I'm convinced that old tapes, laid down in early childhood, can truly hinder our progress in understanding who we are in Christ. I'm beginning to grow out of my old ways of thinking about myself (extremely poor, denigrating self-talk), and about God.

There are two critical takeaways from that letter where we need to learn from to overcome the bondage of legalism and live as liberated children of God. First and foremost, were his distorted beliefs about God and himself, which he assimilated from the environment in which he was raised. When he was born dead in his trespasses and sins, he experienced neither the presence of God in his life nor the knowledge of His ways. So, he learned to live independently of God. Such learning is what the Bible calls the flesh or old nature. Second, he had never experienced genuine repentance.

The moment we were born again, we became new creations in Christ, "... the old things passed away; behold, new things have come" (2 Corinthians 5:17). We were rescued from the kingdom of darkness and transferred to the kingdom of God's beloved Son (see Colossians 1:13). "You are not in the flesh but in the Spirit, if indeed the Spirit of God dwells in you. But if anyone does not have the Spirit of Christ, he does not belong to Him" (Romans 8:9). "For you were formerly darkness, but now you are Light in the Lord; walk as children of Light" (Ephesians 5:8). We are not partially old, and partially new;

partially "in the flesh" and partially "in the Spirit"; and partially darkness and partially light. We will still sin and fall short of God's glory, but "...if anyone sins, we have an Advocate with the Father, Jesus Christ the righteous; and he himself is the propitiation for our sins" (1 John 2:1,2). We also have an adversary who accuses us day and night.

Paul never identifies believers by their old nature; "Therefore from now on we recognize no one according to the flesh" (2 Corinthians 5:16). It is counterproductive to call Christians sinners but expect them to live like saints. No person can consistently behave in a way that is inconsistent with what they believe about themselves. It isn't what we do that determines who we are; it's who we are that determines what we do. So, who are we? John answers, "See how great a love the Father has bestowed upon us, that we would be called children of God; and such we are... Beloved, now we are children of God (1 John 3:1,2).

A pastor who graduated from a prestigious evangelical seminary once wrote a scathing article against me for identifying believers as saints and children of God. So, I called him and asked him why he didn't want to teach his people who they are in Christ. He said, "Because it would take away their motivation to stop sinning." I said, "So you are going to lie to them about who they really are in Christ and motivate them with shame and guilt?" That sounds like the accuser of the brethren. Such messaging not only gives believers a distorted perception of themselves but a distorted concept of God. I have found just the opposite of what he said to be true. Those who are alive and free in Christ strive to live a righteous life as children of God out of gratitude. "Everyone who has this hope fixed upon Him purifies himself, just as He is pure" (1 John 3:3). Every child of God needs to know who they are in Christ and how He meets their critical needs of acceptance, security, and significance as follows:

In Christ

I am Accepted:

John 1:12	I am God's child.
John 15:15	I am Jesus' chosen friend.
Romans 5:1	I have peace with God having been justified.
1 Corinthians 6:17	I am united with the Lord and one with Him in spirit.
1 Corinthians 6:20	I have been bought with a price - I belong to God.
1 Corinthians 12:27	I am a member of Christ's body.
Ephesians 1:1	I am a saint.
Ephesians 1:5	I have been adopted as God's child
Ephesians 2:18	I have direct access to God through the Holy Spirit.

| Colossians 1:14 | I have been redeemed and forgiven of all my sins. |
| Colossians 2:10 | I am complete in Christ. |

I am Secure:

Romans 8:1,2	I am free from condemnation.
Romans 8:28	I am assured that all things work together for good.
Romans 8:31	I am free from any concemning charges against me.
Romans 8:35	I cannot be separated from the love of God.
2 Corinthians 1:21	I have been established, anointed, and sealed by God.
Colossians 3:3	I am hidden with Christ in God.
Philippians 1:6	I am sure that the good work that God has begun in me will be finished.
Philippians 3:20	I am a citizen of heaven.
2 Timothy 1:7	I have not been given a spirit of fear, but of power, love, and a sound mind.
Hebrews 4:16	I can find grace and mercy in time of need.
1John 5:18	I am born of God and the evil one cannot touch me.

I am Significant:

Matthew 5:13	I am the salt and the light of the world.
John 15:5	I am joined to Christ and able to bear fruit.
John 15:16	I have been chosen by Jesus to bear fruit.
Acts 1:8	I am a personal witness of Christ's.
1Corinthians 3:16	I am a temple of God where the Holy Spirit dwells.
2 Corinthians 5:18, 20	I am an ambassador for Christ who gave me the ministry of reconciliation.
2 Corinthians 6:1	I am God's coworker.
Ephesians 2:6	I am seated with Christ in the heavenlies.
Ephesians 2:10	I am God's workmanship.
Ephesians 3:12	I may approach God with freedom and confidence.
Philippians 4:13	I can do all things through Christ who strengthens me.

Some people stay away from church because they don't want a guilt trip. Would you draw near to someone who is going to hammer you for not being perfect? Church is supposed to be the place where you go to get rid of guilt and shame. It has been estimated that half the people in mental institutions could go home if they knew they were completely forgiven, and believers would be at peace if they knew the same. "Therefore, having been justified by faith, we have peace with God through our Lord Jesus Christ" (Romans 5:1). We are not sinners in the hands of an angry God. We are saints in the hands of a loving God. Because of Jesus, "we have boldness and confident access through faith in Him" (Ephesians 3:12). "Therefore, brethren, we have confidence to enter the holy place by the blood of Jesus" (Hebrews 10:19). "Let us draw near with a sincere heart in full assurance of faith, having our hearts sprinkled clean from an evil conscience" (10:22).

The Basis for Acceptance

Christianity can be separated from all other religions by asking one question: On what basis are you accepted? There are no hoops to jump through, no pre-conditions that have to be met. "For by grace you have been saved through faith; and that not of yourselves, it is the gift of God; not as a result of works, so that no one may boast" (Ephesians 2:8,9). "Therefore, accept one another, just as Christ also accepted us to the glory of God" (Romans 15:7). And how did Christ accept us? "God demonstrates His own love for us, in that while we were yet sinners, Christ died for us" (Romans 5:8). We don't labor in the vineyard hoping God will someday accept us. God has already accepted us and that is why we labor in the vineyard.

What qualifies us for God's love? Nothing! God loves us because God is love (1 John 4:8). It is His nature to love us. The love (agape) of God is not dependent upon its object, and that is why God's love is unconditional. Jesus said, "If you love those who love you, what credit is that to you? For even sinners love those who love them" (Luke 6:32). We don't strive to do better hoping that God will someday love us. God loves us and that is why we trust and obey Him.

Struggling believers often wonder, "What experience must I have in order for my identity and position in Christ to be true, because I don't feel loved or forgiven?" There isn't one. The only thing that had to happen, did happen more than 2,000 years ago. We cannot do for ourselves what Christ has already done for us. If we get up in the morning and choose to live according to how we feel, it will probably be a pretty bad day. But if we get up every morning and say, "I deserved hell, but God has forgiven my sins, given me eternal life, and I choose today to walk by faith according to what God says is true in the power of the Holy Spirit," it will all work out in my experience. Trying to make it true by my experience, however, doesn't work.

Some also wonder, "If all that is true, then how come I still think, feel, and behave like I always have?" Because everything you learned about yourself and God is still programmed in your mind, and there is no delete button. That is why Paul wrote, "And do not be conformed to this world, but be transformed by the renewing of your mind" (Romans 12:2). We were all conformed to this world, and we can continue to be so if we believe the same old lies and continue following the ways of the world. So, if we want to be established and grow in our faith, we have to reprogram our minds, but we also better check for "viruses." Computer viruses are not accidental. They have been inserted by disgruntled employees and malicious hackers, which is not unlike the father of lies. Paul says, "I am afraid that, as the serpent deceived Eve by his craftiness, your minds will be led astray from the simplicity and purity of devotion to Christ" (2 Corinthians 11:3).

The seminary student who wrote the letter previously mentioned had a distorted concept of God and himself. He could never measure up to the standards his parents set, and he perceived that God's standards were even higher. But he was also ignorant of the spiritual battle that was waging war against his mind. The accuser would remind him of every way he fell short of God's glory, and he believed it was God who was putting him down.

Accusation versus Conviction

God does, however, convict us of sin. So how can we tell the difference between the Holy Spirit's conviction and Satan's accusations? Paul explains in 2 Corinthians 7:9,10, "I now rejoice, not that you were made sorrowful, but that you were made sorrowful to the point of repentance; for you were made sorrowful according to the will of God, so that you might not suffer loss in anything through us. For the sorrow that is according to the will of God produces repentance without regret, leading to salvation, but the sorrow of the world produces death." Notice that the word sorrow is used for both, but the end result is completely different. Peter must have felt sorrowful when he betrayed Christ, but he repented and became the spokesperson for the early church. Judas betrayed Christ and came under the sorrow of the world and hung himself.

If we have been honest with God in confessing our sins, but still feel pummeled by accusations, rest assured it is not God convicting us. "If we confess our sins, He is faithful and righteous to forgive our sins and to cleanse us from all unrighteousness" (1 John 1:9). Believers are never instructed in the epistles under the new covenant to ask God to forgive us for any sin. Why not? Because we are already forgiven. Christ died to sin once for all (see Romans 6:10). You may wonder, "I know I am forgiven for the sins I have already confessed, but what about the sins I commit in the future?" When Christ died once for all, how many of your sins were future?

Confession simply means to agree with God, and that cleanses us. It is essentially the same as walking in the light, which is living in moral agreement with God. You have confessed when you say, "I did it." It would be a horrible way to live if you think that you are not forgiven unless you have asked God to forgive you for every known sin. First, you are not always aware of every known sin. Second, you would have little assurance of your salvation so you likely go to bed at night worried that you may die and go to hell if you haven't been forgiven of all your sins.

Punishment versus Discipline

A similar distinction should be made between punishment and discipline. Punishment is retroactive, but the purpose of discipline is to correct sinful behavior and attitudes thus superintending future choices. "All discipline for the moment seems not to be joyful, but sorrowful; yet to those who are trained by it, afterward it yields the peaceful fruit of righteousness" (Hebrews 12:11). Godly discipline is a proof of God's love (vs. 7), and those without His discipline are "illegitimate children and not sons" (vs. 8). The punishment we deserved has already fallen on Christ. "There is no fear in love; but perfect love casts out fear, because fear involves punishment, and the one who fears is not perfected in love" (1 John 4:18).

We must also discern the difference between temptation and the testing of our faith. God will test us for the purpose of strengthening our faith. "Let no one say when he is tempted, 'I am being tempted by God'; for God cannot be tempted by evil, and He Himself does not tempt anyone" (James 1:13). But the devil does, and he knows which buttons to push. What may tempt one person may not tempt another. Temptations from without lack power unless there is a corresponding desire within. James continues, "But each one is tempted when he is carried away and enticed by his own lust. Then when lust has conceived, it gives birth to sin; and when sin is accomplished, it brings forth death" (James 1:14,15).

The seminary student mentioned previously had a lot of unresolved personal and spiritual issues and it was only a matter of time before he was swept away by his own lusts. There are two major reasons why struggling believers don't know who they are in Christ. The first is ignorance. If you don't know the truth, it can't set you free. If you think you are a sinner, you will likely sin. The Prophet Hosea said, "My people are destroyed for lack of knowledge" (Hos. 4:6). Lack of repentance is the second reason. Without genuine repentance, most Christians come to church with a lot of baggage from the past. They enter the door, sit their baggage down, hear a good message, pick up their baggage and go back home week after week. That was the case for the following church until the pastor discovered for himself what it means to repent and believe the gospel:

> I thank the Lord for the materials you have created. It is wonderful to use something that works with all sorts of people, with all sorts of problems. I stumbled on to your material a year ago and taught it in a Sunday school class. We also used the material for working with a severely demonized man. In preparing to lead him through The Steps to Freedom in Christ, the elders and I went through them first.

I personally had bondage to sin in my own life, which I have struggled with since childhood that started with my dad's Playboy magazines. My wife also found freedom from her family's occultic background.

I'm in a new church now and without advertising God has sent twelve people to me in one month to go through The Steps. There has been a great work of God in people's hearts. Two of the elders resigned to get their lives straightened out. One has been having an affair for the last two years. I took the other elder and his wife through The Steps last week. He had bondage to pornography, masturbation, and strip joints when he was on business trips. It was wonderful to see both find their freedom, renew and deepen their relationship with God and each other.

One of our Sunday school teachers has been experiencing nighttime terror and demonic dreams. Through God's "chance events," she told my wife about these difficulties. I led her and her husband through The Steps last week. When we came to forgiving others, I had to teach, exhort, and encourage her for over an hour. I physically put a pencil in her hand so she could write down the names of those she needed to forgive. It took another thirty minutes to write the first name. Eventually, she made a decision and went for it.

God is so good! The next Sunday there was so much joy, peace, and freedom on the face of both her and her husband.

Paul's theology is based on who we are in Christ. In the book of Ephesians alone there are forty prepositional statements saying we are "in Christ," "in the Beloved," or "in Him." "Therefore, as you have received Christ Jesus the Lord, so walk *in him*. Having been firmly rooted and being built up *in him* and established in your faith" (Colossians 2:6,7 emphasis added). To grow one has to be connected to the source of life. To be in Christ means that your soul is connected to God, i.e., to be spiritually alive. Paul tells the church in Corinth; "For this reason, I have sent to you Timothy, who is my beloved and faithful child in the Lord, and he will remind you of my ways which are *in Christ*, just as I teach everywhere in every church" (1 Corinthians 4:17 emphasis added). In other words, we have to be firmly rooted in Christ to grow in Christ and live abundantly in Christ. If you don't know who you are in Christ, you aren't firmly rooted in Him.

Little Children versus Young Men

John has another measure of growth; "I am writing to you, little children, because your sins have been forgiven you for His name's sake. I am writing to you, fathers, because you know Him who has been from the beginning. I am writing to you, young men, because you have overcome the evil one" (1 John 2:12,13). In a practical sense, "little children" are free from the penalty of sin, and "young men" are free from the power of sin. How are we going to help believers grow to full stature in Christ if they haven't overcome the evil one? Notice who John is writing to in his first letter; "My little children" (1 John 2:1 see also 2:12; 2:18; 2:24; 3:7; 3:18; 4:4; 5:21). As someone who has been traveling the world for the last forty years helping people overcome the evil one, I would say that the vast majority of believers are still little children. What a tragedy.

Equity, Racism, and Meritocracy

"He (God) will judge the peoples with equity" (Psalm 96:10 ESV). God has no personal biases, and condemns all forms of favoritism, sexism, elitism, and racism. That should also be true for mature believers who have put on the new self "who is being renewed to a true knowledge according to the image of the One who created him – a renewal in which there is no distinction between Greek and Jew, circumcised and uncircumcised, barbarian, Scythian, slave and freeman, but Christ is all, and in all" (Colossians 3:10,11). In other words, there is no social, religious, cultural or racial distinction for those who are in Christ Jesus. In Galatians Paul adds "there is neither male nor female" (Galatians 3:28). God has not eradicated our gender identities. He is saying that all God's children have equal status in the kingdom of God, but we have different roles such as husbands and wives, and different capabilities. The kingdom of God is the most inclusive family in the world. "The death that He died, He died to sin once for all" (Romans 6:10). All who call upon the name of the *Lord* will be saved. We are to accept one another as God has accepted us, and we are to love our enemies, do good to those who hate us, bless those who curse us and pray for those who mistreat us (see Luke 6:27,28).

In the USA, the liberal world order is demanding equity inclusion for every position in life regardless of merit or morality. To be equitable they argue that every position in government and workplace should have an equal number of men and women, and a proportionate number of African Americans, Hispanic, Asian, Caucasians, and any other ethnic group, as well as an equal representation of gays, lesbians, and transgender folks regardless of qualifications. That is a complete departure from the message and method of social justice leader Martin Luther King who longed for the day when people would not be judged by the color of their skin, but rather by the quality of their character and conduct, and he accomplished his goal by holding peaceful demonstrations.

Why does the liberal order hate the Church? Because we believe in righteousness and meritocracy. We invite all, but to be a member of the family of God one has to repent, and believe the gospel, and to be a leader in the Church one has to qualify to be an elder or deacon according to 1 Timothy 3:1-13. "Or do you not know that the unrighteous will not inherit the kingdom of God? Do not be deceived; neither fornicators, nor idolaters, nor adulterers, nor effeminate, nor homosexuals, nor thieves, nor covetous, nor drunkards, nor revilers, nor swindlers, will inherit the kingdom of God" (1 Corinthians 6:9,10).

Liberals believe that we should be more compassionate to those who are marginalized racially and sexually. In one sense Jesus would agree. "Go and learn what this means: I desire compassion, and not sacrifice, for I did not come to call the righteous, but sinners" (Matthew 9:13). However, who is showing more compassion? Those who choose to remove all moral restraints ignoring the long time and eternal consequences of immorality, or believers who help those in bondage to sin repent and find their freedom and new life in Christ?

The challenge for believers in the end times is to be like Jesus who dined with sinners (Luke 5:30,31), but never compromised who He was by participating in their immorality. "Seeing the people, He felt compassion for them, because they were distressed and dispirited like sheep without a shepherd. Then He said to His disciples, 'The harvest is plentiful, but the workers are few. Therefore, beseech the Lord of the harvest to send out workers into His harvest" (Matthew 9:36-38).

Discussion Questions

1. Why do you think legalism is still so present in many churches?
2. Why is it counterproductive to identify believers as sinners instead of saints?
3. How should knowing who you are in Christ affect how you live?
4. How can you gain God's love, or qualify for your position in Christ?
5. If you are a new creation in Christ, why do you still struggle with the same old issues you did as an unbeliever?
6. How can we be transformed by the renewing of our minds and what must we be aware of that could derail us?
7. What is the difference between God convicting us and Satan accusing us?
8. How does the testing of our faith differ from temptation?
9. How easy would it be to fall away from your faith if you didn't know who you are in Christ and hadn't learned to overcome the evil one?
10. How is the church supposed to live with those who call us hypocrites, despise us, and say we need to show more compassion and acceptance?

Chapter Three:
Overcoming Liberalism

Man has deprived himself of the best there is in the world who has deprived himself of this: a knowledge of the Bible . . . This book is the one supreme source of revelation, the revelation of the meaning in life, the nature of God, and the spiritual nature and need of men. It is a book which reveals every man to himself as a distinct moral agent, responsible not to men, not even to those men whom He has put over him in authority, but responsible through his own conscience to his Lord and Maker. Whenever a man sees this vision, he stands up a free man whatever may be the circumstances of his life.

Woodrow Wilson

Woodrow Wilson was a registered democrat and two-term president of the United States. If he were alive today and held the beliefs quoted above, he could not be nominated by his own party.

Not only has politics shifted toward a liberal worldview, but so have the medical, sociological, and psychological professions. Can you name a godly sociologist or psychologist teaching in a secular university or college?

A licensed counselor attended my *Discipleship Counseling* class and introduced himself by saying; "I have been reading about the rise of the New Age and thought I better be prepared in case I come across such people in my practice. I have yet to encounter anything demonic in my fifteen years of counseling." A month later I received a letter admitting that every one of his clients was being deceived and so was he. Why didn't he see it before? First, his education was based on a liberal worldview that explains everything based on rationalism and naturalism. Second, even though he was a believer, he was never taught how to actually resolve personal and spiritual conflicts through genuine repentance and faith in God. His purpose was to explain why people experience difficulties and provide coping skills. Such "paralysis of analysis" doesn't set anyone free. There is no eternal and lasting resolution without Christ. If all we do is explain why people are having difficulties, the devil could not care less and will remain covert. Only when you expose the lie and work toward resolution will you experience any opposition.

After a conference on "Resolving Personal and Spiritual Conflicts" a man told me that he had just been accepted into a secular Doctor of Psychology program. "Are you suggesting that I shouldn't go?" he asked. I said, "I'm not questioning how God is leading you, but would I personally commit five years of my life and spend at least $200,000 to learn how to help others live their lives independently of God and try to explain how their needs can be met without Christ?" "I never thought about it that way," he said. I think everyone should consider that question, and take seriously Psalm 1:1, "How blessed is the man who does not walk in the counsel of the wicked, nor stand in the path of sinners, nor sit in the seat of scoffers."

Elemental Spirits

After explaining that believers need to be firmly rooted in Christ to grow in Christ, Paul wrote, "See to it that no one takes you captive through philosophy and empty deception, according to the elementary principles of the world, rather than according to Christ" (Colossians 2:8). "Elementary principles" is the Greek word *stoicheia,* which other translations render as "elemental spirits" (RSV/NEB) and "ruling spirits" (TEV). According to Greek scholar, Dr. Clinton Arnold, "The interpretation of *stoicheia* as personal spiritual entities is the most compelling view. Consequently, this interpretation has commanded the consent of the majority of commentators in the history of the interpretation of the passages. This view is based partly on the widespread usage of *stoicheia* for astral spirits in the second and third centuries."[11] This interpretation makes even more sense in Galatians. "So also, we, while we were children, were held in bondage under the elemental things (*stoicheia*) of the world" (Galatians 4:3). "But now you have come to know God, or rather to be known by God, how is it that you can turn back again to the weak and worthless elemental things (*stoicheia*) to which you desire to be enslaved all over again" (Galatians 4:9). "Things" don't lie to us, but the father of lies and his demons do. People are in bondage to the lies they believe, whether those lies come from worldly philosophies, empty deception, traditions of men, or deceiving spirits. We are transformed by the renewing of our minds, but you can't renew the lies of deceiving spirits. You have to renounce those lies and tell the enemy to leave.

The brain is the capstone of the central nervous system and is governed by the mind. The hardware (the brain) doesn't tell the software (the mind) what to do. It's the other way around. We don't do anything without first thinking it, and emotions are essentially a product of our thoughts. The problem is people are reticent to share what is going on in their minds, and we can't read each other's minds. Unless they have the courage to share what their troubling thoughts are, all we see are damaged emotions and poor behavior. I have met with thousands who are struggling with condemning and blasphemous thoughts, and some will refer to such thoughts as one or more "voices." Secular psychiatrists and psychologists are dealing with clients who have similar symptoms as well, but they will likely understand that to be a chemical imbalance.

Honest questions need to be asked. How can a chemical produce a personality and a thought? How can neurotransmitters randomly create a personality and a thought that one is opposed to thinking? There is no natural explanation for that, but what you will likely see here is: "I prescribed an anti-psychotic medication and the voices stopped." Sure, and so did almost everything else in terms of cognition. All that does is narcotize the brain. Take away the medication and the voices are back, so nothing was resolved. Silencing those condemning thoughts is the primary reason why people drink and take drugs. They have no mental peace.

The wife of a seminary professor struggled with pneumonia that was later found to be cancerous. She became phobic and asked to see me. This lovely Christian lady said, "Neil, I'm not sure I'm a Christian." I asked her why she was even questioning that. She said, "When I go to church, I have these blasphemous thoughts about God." I asked, "Did you want to think those thoughts, and did you make a conscious choice to think those thoughts? "No," she said. "Then why do you believe those were your thoughts?" Within a half hour she was free from those lies, being the mature believer, she actually was. She had concluded that if those thoughts were hers, then she must not be a Christian, and that is why she was so fearful. She was facing the prospect of dying without the assurance of salvation.

Truth Revealed

Truth is what sets us free, and it is divinely revealed in three ways. First, Jesus is the ultimate revelation because He is the Truth. "He is the radiance of His glory and the exact representation of His nature and upholds all things by the word of His power" (Hebrews 1:3). God is the Creator of all things visible and invisible and therefore the ultimate reality. Nothing exists without Him. "For since the creation of the world His invisible attributes, His eternal power and divine nature, have been clearly seen, being understood through what has been made, so that they are without excuse" (Romans 1:20). Second, we can know what is true through general revelation. General revelation can be observed through our natural senses and validated through empirical research. This is the only truth the secular world knows and is the basis for secular education.

Finally, there is special revelation, which is the Word of God. Jesus prayed, "Sanctify them in truth; Your word is truth" (John 17:17). "The heavens are telling of the glory of God, and their expanse is declaring the work of His hands" (Psalm 19:1). That verse refers to general revelation, and verses 7-9 refers to special revelation (emphasis added):

> The law of the Lord is perfect, *restoring the soul*: the testimony of the Lord is sure, *making wise the simple*. The precepts of the Lord are right, *rejoicing the heart*; the commandment of the Lord is pure, *enlightening the eyes*; the fear of the Lord is clean, *enduring forever*; the judgments of the Lord are true; they are righteous altogether.

Even in some Christian circles empirical research is given equal or greater significance than divine revelation. There are four reasons why general revelation is insufficient to know all that is true without Scripture.

First, special revelation is authoritative, whereas general revelation (nature) is illustrative. Without special revelation to explain life and its meaning, we have no recourse but to fall back on philosophical speculation. Research may reveal what is, but it can't explain why.

Second, empirical research leaves out the reality of the spiritual world by its own definition. God does not submit to our methods of investigation or verification. We cannot scientifically prove the existence of God to the satisfaction of the skeptic. The Bible makes no attempt to prove itself. Those who come to God "must believe that He is and that He is a rewarder of those who seek Him" (Hebrews 11:6). Rest assured that the god of this world is not going to cooperate with our research methods. Satan operates under the cloak of deception and will not voluntarily reveal himself for our benefit.

Third, the rational process of verification is always interpreted through the grid of our own cultural, educational, and personal experiences. We naturally interpret what we observe from our own perspective. Wisdom is understanding life from God's perspective.

Finally, God intended general revelation to be evaluated through the grid of Scripture, not through the grid of a godless worldview. A skeptic and a mature Christian can analyze the same data and draw different conclusions. Somebody hearing voices would likely be diagnosed as schizophrenic by secular counselors, whereas I would never assume that. To illustrate, read the following email I received:

> For years, ever since I was a teenager (I am now 36), I had these "voices" in my head. There were four in particular and sometimes what seemed like loud choruses of them. When the subject of schizophrenia would come up on television or in a magazine, I would think to myself, "I know I am not schizophrenic, but what is this in my head? I was tortured, mocked, jeered, and every single thought I had was second-guessed. Consequently, I had zero self-esteem. I often used to wish the voices would be quiet and I always wondered if other people had this as well and if it was "common."

> When I started to learn from you about taking every thought captive to the obedience of Christ and read about other people's experiences with these voices, I came to recognize them for what they were, and I was able to make them leave. That was an amazing and beautiful thing, to be fully quiet in

my mind after so many years of torment. I do not need to explain further all the wonderful things that come with this freedom of the mind, it is a blessing you seem to know well.

With a secular worldview, doctors, psychiatrists, and psychologists can only make use of natural resources and human reasoning. Secular psychology makes sense if there are only humans living in a natural world. If doctors correctly diagnose patients with a mental or emotional illness during a fifteen-minute appointment, what will they do? They will prescribe medication. I am not against the proper use of medication. Taking a pill to cure our bodies is commendable, but taking a pill to cure our souls is deplorable and may God grant us the wisdom to know the difference.

If we fully understood natural law (what God has created) and divine revelation they would be academically compatible, but our knowledge of both is incomplete. Science is humanity's attempt to understand natural law. Theology is the Christian's attempt to systematize truth. As I have matured in Christ my theology has changed. Truth hasn't changed, but my understanding of truth has, because I am seeing truth more and more from God's perspective. The scientist and the theologian may be at odds with each other due to our limited understanding, but natural law and divine revelation are in perfect agreement, because God is the origin of both.

The Politicization of Science

The liberal worldview places a great emphasis on "following the science", but science is being politicized to fit a particular narrative. True science does not support the liberal agenda. No scientific study, for example, has identified a gene or combination of genes that means that some are born alcoholics or gay. We are genetically predisposed to certain characteristics, but that doesn't make anyone an alcoholic or gay. Our DNA clearly indicates that we are born male and female. Pharmaceutical companies have made billions of dollars and continue to pedal drugs for psychosomatic problems that can be resolved through repentance and lifestyle changes.

The politicization of the World Health Organization (WHO) and the Center for Disease Control (CDC) has eroded the credibility of science and the medical profession. The World Bank has established ESG (Environment, Social, and Governance) ratings to determine which countries they will support financially and to give guidance on which companies investors should choose. Carbon footprint is their leading environmental concern, and their intention is to drastically cut the use of things deemed to cause greenhouse gases, such as fossil fuel, cows (because of their flatulence), and fertilizer. Christians believe in science and absolutely agree that we should be good stewards of the planet and its environment, but ESG ratings include criteria for "Social" and "Governance" too which means that investment depends not only on environmental issues but on, for example, equity inclusion.

The great danger is that this could easily become a tool to control the political agenda and indeed a country's entire population rather than helping the environment – and some believe that is already happening. Countries and companies that don't support equity inclusion will simply not get funded and so cannot function. If you disagree with the approach you are labeled as being against "science," and perhaps perceived to be racist or homophobic. Yet those behind it appear to continue to drive the most cars, take the most flights and live in the biggest houses, and it's difficult not to wonder whether there is an agenda to entrench godless thinking at the heart of government. Imagine one of them standing on a platform with a bullhorn saying, "We will give all of you jobs, and make sure all your physical and medical needs will be provided for. Just trust us."

Rethinking Our Worldview

Fernando Garzon's father came to the States to attend medical school and later married a U.S. citizen. Fernando was born in the United States and brought up in a Christian home. Here is his story:

> I became a Christian when I was sixteen years old and immediately got involved in Bible studies and Christian fellowships. These were good experiences for me, furnishing much love and support. In college, I began encountering many friends who clearly needed emotional healing. They went through deliverance, and prayer sessions, and studied their Bibles, but they didn't seem to get better. That bothered me, because that was basically all I knew from a spiritual perspective about how they might get help. I began asking questions that most of my Christian friends couldn't answer.
>
> After college, I began working at a psychiatric hospital to learn more about helping people. I eventually went to Fuller Seminary and received my doctorate in clinical psychology. I learned a great deal about what causes emotional stress and learned strategies for helping people cope. Unfortunately, I didn't learn how to answer my initial questions about why spiritual interventions like deliverance, bible study, and prayer had such limited success! Without clear answers, I began to de-emphasize the role of the spiritual in the healing process and focus more on secular techniques. I would pray for my clients occasionally, but that was about the limit of my explicitly Christian interventions.
>
> I had plenty of secular techniques at my disposal, but few if any concrete Christian intervention strategies. I started to ask myself serious questions as a Christian psychologist. Suppose someone videoed one of my counseling sessions and that of a secular therapist who is well-trained in how

to handle religious issues in treatment. Would somebody watching both videos be able to tell who the Christian therapist is and who is the sensitively trained secular therapist? There would be very little difference other than an occasional opening and closing prayer. That was unsatisfactory for me. If a Christian client wanted Jesus actively integrated into treatment, I had little to offer.

I asked the Lord to show me concrete Christian intervention strategies, and I was led to Neil's first two books, *Victory Over the Darkness* and *The Bondage Breaker*. These books espoused approaches compatible with well-researched clinical psychology called cognitive therapy, yet they were much broader in addressing a variety of areas consistent with a biblical worldview. These books opened my eyes to an entirely different way of conceptualizing spiritual influences in therapy. They certainly were not the typical deliverance ministries I had been exposed to in my early Christian days. They had something more. Demons were not the major problem; rather, root issues and unresolved conflicts in our lives were the major problem. Based on my previous experiences (and now as a Christian psychologist), I could readily agree with that.

My journey was quite different from Fernando's. My ministry started with a good theological education, but I wasn't fully equipped to help people resolve their problems. I believed that Christ was the answer, and that truth would set people free, but I didn't see the kind of results the Bible seemed to indicate. People had problems that I really didn't have answers for. When I was called to teach at Talbot School of Theology, I went there searching for answers.

I offered a Master of Theology elective on spiritual warfare. I felt like I was a second grader teaching first graders. Despite my limited knowledge and experience the class grew from 18 the first year, to 23 the next year, then 35, then 65, then 150 and finally 250 students took a one-week intensive class which included local pastors and Christian workers. I started seeing the lives of students literally change as they discovered who they were in Christ and after they had resolved their personal and spiritual conflicts through genuine repentance and faith in God.

During those learning years, God sent many wounded Christians with all kinds of problems to see me for personal counseling. Initially, I got stuck more times than not and didn't know where to go next. So, I would stop and pray, because God said that if we lacked wisdom, we should ask for it. I told the inquirers that I didn't know what the answer was to their problem, but I believed God did. So, I prayed out loud in their presence asking God for guidance. I remember sitting in silence with one inquirer for several minutes, waiting upon the Lord.

Then one day the thought occurred to me that I was asking God to tell me so I could tell them. That would make me a medium, and Paul wrote in 1 Timothy 2:5, "For there is one God, and one mediator also between God and men, the man Christ Jesus." Since we are not called to function like a medium, I thought, "Why don't I have them pray and ask God themselves?" Every Christian is a child of God, and we all have the same access to our Heavenly Father.

I believe in intercessory prayer, but that is never intended by God to replace the individual's responsibility to pray. To illustrate, suppose you have two sons, and your younger son is always going to his older brother with a request, "Go ask Dad if I can have ten dollars so I can go to the movies tonight?" Would that be okay for you as a parent to have a second-hand relationship with one of your own children? Do you think our Heavenly Father wants anything different for all His children?

One afternoon I wrote out some simple petitions that the inquirer could pray, and I tried it in counseling. I was totally amazed at what happened. God showed them. Those prayers, along with instructions, became *The Steps to Freedom in Christ*[12] (*The Steps*), which are being used all over the world. It is a repentance process that directly connects the inquirer to God through prayer. Whenever I attempt to help another individual there are always three who are present, and there is a role that God, and only God, can play in the other person's life. I can't set a captive free, and I can't mend broken hearts, but God can, and that is why Jesus came according to Luke 4:17-19:

> The book of the Prophet Isaiah was handed to him. And he opened the book and found the place where it was written, "The Spirit of the Lord is upon me, because he anointed me to preach the Gospel to the poor. He sent me to proclaim release to the captives, and recovery of sight to the blind, to set free those who are oppressed, to proclaim the favorable year of the Lord.

Psychology is by definition a study of the soul. I am certainly not against psychology, but I am not in agreement with secular psychology, just as I am not in agreement with liberal theology. The general theory of secular counseling is not complicated. The goal is to develop skills like empathy, congruence, concreteness, etc., which are just good pastoral skills. The purpose is to gain the client's confidence, draw out their life story, explain why they are not feeling and doing so well, offer better ways of thinking and living, and then help them cope with their situation.

Secular psychology can't accomplish any more than that because they have no Gospel and no God to lead and empower them. The difference between secular and Christian psychology is not just a question of the message, but also one of methodology. I can't fix your past, and neither does God. He sets you free from it. Most people are reticent to disclose their innermost being just to gain some understanding of why they are so messed up, but almost everyone will if God is convicting them for the purpose of resolving their conflicts.

God knows everything about us, and He is the only One who can heal us and set us free, so why aren't we including Him in the process? When I learned to do so, my ministry was transformed. It was no longer a question of just learning better skills and counseling techniques. I began to understand that Christian counseling is an encounter with God. Now I begin a session with another by asking what they are struggling with and listening to their story. I have learned over the years that the presenting problem is almost always a symptom of an underlying root issue, which God already knows. Then I ask, "Would you like to resolve this?" Nobody has ever said no. Then I say, "With your permission, I would like to lead you through *The Steps to Freedom in Christ*." Again, nobody has ever said no.

The Steps are mainly petitions that the inquirer prays asking God to reveal to their minds issues that are critical in terms of their relationship with God, including false guidance, deception, unforgiveness, rebellion, pride, sin, and family ties.[13]

Suppose a twenty-year-old college student is depressed and struggles with bitterness toward his father. He goes to see his pastor who should know that forgiving his father is essential to have an intimate relationship with God. So, he explains what forgiveness is and how to forgive from the heart, and the student chooses to do so. That will resolve a major conflict in his life, but is that enough? No, that will only be the tip of the iceberg in the majority of cases. If the college student prayed, asking God to reveal to his mind whom he needed to forgive, his father would likely be the first person mentioned, but chances are twenty other names would surface as well. How much has the pastor helped him if he only forgave his father and not the others? Additionally, since he is twenty years old, what are the chances that he has been sexually active, or struggling with rebellion, or pride? The point is, God loves that boy and knows every issue that is keeping him from having an intimate relationship. If we include God in the process those issues will surface when the inquirer goes through *The Steps*.

I am always amazed by what comes up when I lead people through *The Steps*. I regularly hear people say, "I have never shared this with anyone ever before." That is not because I am a good counselor, and they are not sharing the information with me just to gain some understanding. They are sharing it with God to resolve their personal and spiritual conflicts. As a facilitator you never have to point out their sins, because God "...will convict the world concerning sin and righteousness and judgment" (John 16:8). When the conviction comes from God, the power to change comes with it. Nobody wants to expose their dark secrets and shame to another, but God lovingly surfaces those issues, and they are grateful for it when the session is over. I have never seen anyone regret this encounter with God, because "The will of God produces a repentance *without regret*" (2 Corinthians 7:10, emphasis added).

Discipleship Counseling is a ministry of reconciliation. You are helping them remove the barriers to their intimacy with God. To illustrate how effective this process is, Judith King, a Christian therapist, conducted three pilot studies on participants who attended a "Living Free in Christ"[14] conference and were led through *The Steps* during the conference.

The first study involved thirty participants who took a ten-item questionnaire before completing *The Steps*. The questionnaire was re-administered three months after their participation. The questionnaire assessed levels of depression, anxiety, inner conflict, tormenting thoughts, and addictive behaviors. The second and third study involved fifty-five and twenty-one participants who took a twelve-item questionnaire before completing *The Steps* and were then re-administered three months later. The following table illustrates the percentage of improvement:

	Depression	Anxiety	Inner Conflict	Tormenting Thoughts	Addictive Behavior
Pilot Study 1:	64%	58%	63%	82%	52%
Pilot Study 2:	47%	44%	51%	58%	43%
Pilot Study 3:	52%	47%	48%	57%	39%

Research was also conducted at Tyler and Oklahoma City conferences by a doctoral student at Regent University under the supervision of Dr. Fernando Garzon. A personal session was offered to those who couldn't process *The Steps* on their own with a trained facilitator. They were given a pre-test before a *Steps* session and a post-test three months later with the following results given in percentage of improvement:

	Oklahoma City, OK	Tyler, TX
Depression	44%	52%
Anxiety	45%	44%
Fear	48%	49%
Anger	36%	55%

Tormenting Thoughts ▲	51%	27%
Negative Habits	48%	43%
Sense of Self-Worth	52%	40%

In the preceding research, all the counseling was done by trained lay people. *The Steps* enable people to submit to God and resist the devil (see James 4:7). We have learned how to do that without ever losing control in a session, even in the most severe demonic cases. The process is a combination of discipleship and counseling, which I believe are the same ministries in the Bible. If you are a good Christian disciple, you are also a good Christian counselor and vice versa.

Beyond Cognitive Behavioral Therapy

Cognitive Behavioral Therapy (CBT) is the most accepted method of counseling in the United States, both secular and Christian. The concept is not complicated. People are doing what they are doing and feeling what they are feeling, because of what they have chosen to think and/or believe. Therefore, if you want to change what people are doing and feeling, what should you do? You should help them change what they believe or think. Essentially, CBT is repentance which literally means "a change of mind." However, it is often incomplete.

When I taught a Doctor of Ministry class at Regent University, Dr. Garzon asked if I would be willing to conduct research on the participating students. The class also included Doctor of Psychology Students and Master of Divinity students numbering in the forties. The class was on discipleship counseling, lasting nine hours every day for five days. They were led through *The Steps* near the end of the class. Keep in mind that these students do not represent the general population, since they were all committed Christians doing graduate work. Besides, most students enroll in a class to fulfill a degree requirement and hopefully gain some insight to enhance their ministry, but not necessarily to have their life changed.

The students took tests on Monday morning at the beginning of the class, and Friday afternoon at the end of the class. They also took the same tests three weeks later to see if any gains were sustained. Every scale was statistically significant. Dr. Garzon reported the results in a paper that was published by the Journal of Psychology and Theology, which is published by Rosemead Graduate School of Psychology at Biola University. They asked Dr. Garzon how I could explain such results. In other words, what was I doing beyond cognitive behavioral therapy? That is a fair question. Isn't it just CBT if I taught them the truth, and they believed the truth and the truth set them free?

When Dr. Garzon related the question to me I said, "Three issues come to mind." First, CBT as practiced by Christian and secular therapists does bring about brief changes in mood and behavior, but it doesn't change who the client is. Christians should be more effective since they have the truth of God's Word. However, even if you use the Word of God in CBT without the life of Christ, you will not be effective in producing lasting change. When I say the life of Christ, I am not referring to the physical manifestation of God 2,000 years ago, I am talking about the life of Christ indwelling every believer.

Second, you will not see the kind of results mentioned in the preceding research when applying CBT if you don't take into account the reality of the spiritual world. If people are paying attention to deceiving spirits, they cannot resolve that by just submitting to God without also resisting the devil.

Third, I am not the Wonderful Counselor. I didn't set that class free, and neither did *The Steps*. God set them free as they chose to repent and believe the truth. If you were lost in a maze, I don't think you would want a 'mazeologist' to explain to you the intricacies of the maze and give you coping skills to survive. Nor would you want a legalistic preacher scolding you for getting lost in the first place. I think you would want to know the way, the truth, and the life.

We are all in this mess because of the fall. We just have to be convinced that reconciliation with God is the answer. Many people have given up on God because they have never been fully reconciled to Him through faith and genuine repentance. Liberal churches have turned to the natural and social sciences for enlightenment.

Recovery in Christ

The popular "Twelve Step" program began with the Oxford Group and originally had six steps. It was a Christ-centered Presbyterian program that was bearing fruit. Others took note and wanted to use the program but didn't believe in God. Six more steps were added, and the concept of God was replaced by a "higher power." As a result, it ceased to be a Christian ministry though many Christian ministries use it to good effect.

The turbulent 1960s produced a number of Christians needing help to overcome addictive behaviors, and the church wasn't equipped to respond. Just as we tried to "Christianize" secular psychology, we tried to "Christianize" secular recovery programs, but with the programs came a lot of beliefs that weren't consistent with Scripture. Let me name a few that are still in play. First, participants are instructed to "work the program, because the program works." There is no program that can set anyone free. The reason the original six steps worked was because of Jesus, not because of the program.

Second, secular programs teach that alcoholism is a disease and incurable. Once you are an alcoholic, you will always be an alcoholic. That is bad theology that sounds like "once a sinner, always a sinner," which isn't true either. We were sinners, but now we are saints who sin. You can't expect to live a righteous life if your core identity is still sin. Blaming it on a disease is supposed to make someone feel better, but for many, it absolves them from assuming their responsibility to live a righteous life. Sin is not a disease. Sin is what separates us from God, and sin keeps us from an intimate relationship with Him when we become His children.

Third, Christians shouldn't introduce themselves by their flesh patterns such as, "Hi, I'm Neil and I am an addict, or alcoholic, or co-addict, or co-alcoholic." The struggling Christian should say, "Hi, I'm Neil, I'm a child of God who is struggling with poor choices and bad behavior, but I am learning how to win the battle for my mind." Reinforcing a failure identity is counterproductive to becoming complete in Christ.

Fourth, sobriety is not the right goal. If abstinence is the goal, then Ephesians 5:18 would read, "Be not drunk with wine, therefore stop drinking." Instead, it reads, "...be filled with the Spirit..." "But I say, walk by the Spirit, and you will not carry out the desire of the flesh" (Galatians 5:16). I will talk more about what it means to "walk by the Spirit" in a later chapter. If you take alcohol away from alcoholics, you will be left with "dry drunks" who will likely be more miserable than they were before. You just took away their means of coping without giving them a replacement. Try taking a bone away from a dog, and you will have a dog fight. Try throwing the dog a steak, and it will spit out the old bone.

Fifth, some secular programs have a dual diagnosis when a multiple diagnosis is the reality. Show me anyone who is addicted to anything, and I will show you someone who is depressed, anxious, fearful, ashamed, guilty, angry, and bitter with a poor sense of worth. You cannot resolve all that plus their relational problems at home by simply taking away their chemical of choice. Additionally, most people who are seeking treatment for chemical addiction are also sexually addicted. In most cases, sexual addiction isn't even addressed, and it is more difficult to overcome.

Finally, if you attend one of these self-help groups you will hear statements like, "You have to get rid of that stinking thinking," or "Don't pay attention to that 'committee' in your head." Secular recovery programs and unfortunately most Christian programs are not taking into account the reality of the spiritual world, and don't acknowledge or understand the spiritual battle going on for their minds. Have you ever tried not to think of sexual thoughts or tempting thoughts? Did that work?

The point I am trying to make is that we have a whole God who deals with the whole person, and He takes into account reality all of the time. As Christian doctors, psychologists, nutritionists, and pastors we should think holistically from a biblical perspective. Western medicine has focused primarily on the physical cure of illnesses and patching up physical wounds. Curing an illness, however, does not necessarily promote good health, just like trying not to think bad thoughts doesn't produce good mental health. The majority of illnesses are psychosomatic and such illnesses can be resolved through genuine repentance and faith in God.

Discussion Questions

1. What potentially could be wrong with pursuing a secular and terminal degree in sociology or psychology?
2. What (or whom) are the elementary principles or things of this world?
3. Why do many Christian pastors, counselors, and disciplers glibly accept the diagnosis and medical prescriptions of the secular world?
4. What can and should we learn from general revelation? How is that different from special revelation and how should they be juxtaposed?
5. How does your experience relate to Fernando's experience and that of the author?
6. Why can't intercessory prayer for another accomplish as much as individuals assuming their responsibility to pray?
7. Why must we include God in the process of helping them resolve their personal and spiritual conflicts?
8. What is Cognitive Behavioral Therapy (CBT)? How does that relate to repentance? What are the limitations of CBT if God isn't the initiator, and the spiritual world is ignored?
9. Why are secular recovery programs insufficient for complete recovery in Christ?
10. What do you think will happen to those believers who struggle with addictive behavior, depression, anxiety, fear, and anger if the Church cannot provide a Christ-centered and holistic answer?

Chapter Four: Overcoming False Prophets and Teachers

The false apostles looked good on the surface, but underneath they robbed the soul. Indeed, they took money as well, though they were careful to conceal that as much as possible... An angel of light is one who is free to speak because he stands close to God. This is what the devil pretends to be.[15]

Chrysostom

These illusions are apparitions of that spirit who seeks to ensnare unhappy souls in the deceptive rites of a multitude of false gods and to turn them aside from true worship of the true God, by whom alone they can be purified and healed.[16]

Augustine

The worldviews in this chapter and the next place more emphasis on the reality of the spiritual world and the ministries of deliverance and inner healing. Pentecostalism grew out of the Azusa Street revival and later the Welsh revival in the early twentieth century. As any new movement is, it was met with resistance and much of it centered on the gifts of tongues and prophecy. Concerning the gift of tongues there were those who said, "you must have," and those who said, "you can't have," and neither position reflects the biblical balance taught by the apostle Paul, "all don't speak with tongues do they" (1 Corinthians 12:30)? It is a rhetorical question, but the obvious answer is no. Then Paul added, "do not forbid to speak in tongues" (1 Corinthians 14:39). That seems pretty clear to me. The omniscient God must have known there would be this potential division, so He clarified the proper use of both gifts in 1 Corinthians 14.

Paul provides another balancing perspective in 1 Thessalonians 5:19-21, "Do not quench the Spirit; do not despise prophetic utterances. But examine everything carefully; hold fast to that which is good." There are those who despise prophetic utterances and those who won't examine anything. That seems pretty clear as well. "But God has so composed the body, giving more abundant honor to that member which lacked, so that there may be no division in the body, but that the members may have the same care for one another" (1 Corinthians 13:24,25).

During a dinner conversation with a church staff team in Venezuela, the pastor sheepishly commented, "I guess I'm now considered to be an apostle." Some international figure had appointed him as such, and he seemed uncomfortable with the idea. An identical experience happened with a pastor in Colombia, South America. Both these Pentecostal pastors were credible leaders with fruitful ministries, and in no way would I consider these two men to be false prophets, but does the label of "apostle" aptly fit them? They were in a position of leadership over Pentecostal churches. Throughout church history they would be considered bishops or district superintendents who oversee pastors.

Understanding the term apostle and distinguishing the gift of prophecy from the role of a prophet are matters the Church in the twenty-first century must address. Nobody wants to limit the Lord from speaking to His people in these critical days, but if we don't ask important questions, some may come under the influence of false prophets and teachers.

The Church has never historically taught that there would be more apostles than the ones selected by Christ including the Apostle Paul. None of the church fathers nor the reformers claimed such titles for themselves during the Reformation. While we may not agree on ecclesiastical titles and positions, we must heed clear warnings from Scripture. The place of the church in God's unfolding plan is summarized in Ephesians 2:19-22:

> So then you are no longer strangers and aliens, but you are fellow citizens with the saints, and are of God's household, having been built upon the foundation of the apostles and prophets, Christ Jesus Himself being the corner stone, in whom the whole building, being fitted together is growing into a holy temple in the Lord; in whom you also are being built together into a dwelling of God in the Spirit.

The means by which God has communicated this redemptive plan is revealed in the Bible through the prophets and the apostles. The ultimate revelation of God is Jesus, who is the cornerstone of the church. "God, after he spoke long ago to the fathers in prophets in many portions and in many ways, in these last days has spoken to us in His Son, whom he appointed heir of all things through whom also he made all things" (Hebrews 1:1,2).

Tests of a True Prophet

Old Testament prophets were messengers of God, and they never spoke presumptuously. God said to Moses, "Now then go, and I, even I, will be with your mouth, and teach you what you are to say" (Exodus 4:12). "I will raise up a prophet from among their countrymen like you, and I will put my words in his mouth, and he shall speak to them all that I command him" (Deuteronomy 18:18). God said to Jeremiah, "Behold, I have put my words in your mouth" (Jeremiah 1:9). And Ezekiel received this instruction: "But you shall speak my words to them whether they listen or not, for they are rebellious" (Ezekiel 2:7).

When Old Testament prophets spoke, it was: "Thus saith the Lord." They spoke with authority because it was God's message, not a message from a man. One test of a true prophet was that he was never wrong (Deuteronomy 18:20-22). People needed to discern whether a person was a true or false prophet, but they were not left with the responsibility of deciding what part of a prophecy was right and what part was wrong. If any part was wrong, the prophet was false. Unfortunately, they listened to a lot of false prophets and stoned a lot of true prophets because they didn't want to change their unrighteous ways of living.

Old Testament history ends 400 years before Christ, a period during which the world was without a prophetic voice. Then the Word became flesh and dwelt among us (John 1:14). Planet earth was about to hear from God, but this time through His Son. After a year of public ministry, Jesus appointed twelve disciples who were identified as apostles. They were not called prophets because the word 'prophet' at the time had come to mean any messenger, secular or sacred.

Since the closing of the Canon in the fourth century, the historical church has never considered any others to be prophets and apostles who speak with the absolute authority of "Thus saith the Lord." So why are some identifying their leaders as apostles and prophets, of whom many are self-appointed? Are they just redefining terms, or are they seeking to enhance their status by giving themselves or receiving a lofty title? If that is the case, it has happened before as revealed by Irenaeus in the second century:

> He will judge false prophets, who have not received the gift of prophecy from God. They are not possessed of the fear of God. Instead, either for the sake of vainglory, or with a view to some personal advantage (or acting in some other way under the influence of a wicked spirit), they pretend to utter prophecies, while at the same time they lie against God.[17]

Defining Terms

Some groups understand Ephesians 4:11 to be teaching a five-fold ministry of apostles, prophets, evangelists, pastors, and teachers. However, their definition of an apostle varies. Some have redefined the word apostle to mean someone who has been sent by God to offer visionary leadership. Others use the term apostle for someone who is authoritatively ushering in a new order. The latter may view the Church as dead or apostate.

While I agree that the Church desperately needs renewal, there is nothing wrong with the foundation that has already been laid, and there will not be another. Martin Luther saw the same need and courageously called for repentance, but he never saw himself as an apostle or the need to bring in a new order. Scripture teaches that the foundation has already been laid (past tense) by the apostles and prophets. God is still working today, as He has in the past, through people called into ministry.

Prophets like Isaiah and apostles like Paul were people who had a God-ordained appointment. The church has gifted people, and the gift of prophecy functions like other gifts within the church. However, the New Testament gift of prophecy is different from the Old Testament office of prophet. Having the gift of prophecy does not make anyone a prophet. Christians are children of God, supernaturally gifted to help build one another up to live righteously. God builds upon the foundation that has already been laid by the apostles and prophets by giving us evangelists and pastor/teachers (Ephesians 4:11,12). Evangelists and pastor/teachers are people ordained by God to equip the saints so they (the saints) can do the work of ministry.

Although Satan has been disarmed, the kingdom of darkness is still operating during the church age. Along with true evangelists, pastors, teachers, and others gifted by God for ministry, Satan has his own parade of false prophets, teachers, and messiahs. Whenever God sows a seed, the devil sows a counterfeit. Therefore, let's examine Scripture to learn how to identify false prophets and teachers. Please keep in mind that many leaders who have been given the title of Apostle or Prophet are not false apostles or prophets, unless they fail the tests given below.

I appeal to this segment of the church to reconsider those titles for the sake of unity. Such titles do not enhance their status with the majority of the church. In fact, they tend to close the door to possible inclusion in Christian circles other than their own, and thus limits the potential of many good leaders.

Deuteronomy 18:20-22 explains that if an alleged prophet spoke presumptuously (i.e., his own thoughts, not God's), the prophet was to die. If what he said didn't come true, he was a false prophet. That test works when the words of the prophet predict some future event. Predicting the future is not the primary purpose of a true prophet. A prophet was more like an Old Testament preacher who proclaimed the truth and called for people to repent. Prophecy literally means to tell forth. It can mean to tell before time, or it can mean to tell before people. For instance, the Jewish arrangement of the Old Testament did not include Daniel among the prophets because he didn't preach, even though the book of Daniel has many prophetic messages concerning the future.

Deuteronomy 13:1-3 identifies an even more insidious aspect of false prophets:

> If a prophet or a dreamer of dreams arises among you and gives you a sign or a wonder, and the sign or the wonder comes true, concerning which he spoke to you, saying, "Let us go after them," you shall not listen to the words of that prophet or that dreamer of dreams: for the Lord your God is testing you to find out if you love the Lord your God with all your heart and with all your soul.

In this case, the signs and wonders came true, but their purpose was to lead people away from God to serve other gods. These dreamers of dreams were rebellious at heart (Deuteronomy 13:5). They use signs and wonders to lure people off the true path, and a gullible public blindly follows, because they accept anything supernatural as being from God. The intention is to draw us away from the Word of God. In Old Testament times God considered their evil so great that He required their death by the hands of their own family members (Deuteronomy 13:4-10).

False Prophets

Jeremiah 23:21-32 contains the most extensive analysis of false prophets in the Old Testament:

> I did not send these prophets, but they ran. I did not speak to them, but they prophesied. But if they had stood in my council, then they would have announced my words to my people and would have turned them back from their evil way and from the evil of their deed" (verses 21,22)

Notice two errors. They were not sharing God's words, and what they were sharing did not turn the people away from their evil deeds. True prophets only announced God's words, and their primary purpose was to disclose unrighteousness. They called people back to the moral standards of the law and declared the way of the Lord.

False prophets would share their dreams (Jeremiah 23:25), but Jeremiah explains their relative value (23:28-29), "The prophet who has a dream may relate his dream but let him who has my word speak my word in truth. What does straw have in common with grain?" declares the LORD. "Is not my word like fire?" declares the LORD, "and like a hammer which shatters a rock?"

Straw has no nutritional value and so is only good for bedding, but grain does. God says their dreams were like straw, but His Word is like grain, and we will grow only when we devour God's Word. When we substitute the chaff of dreams for the grain of biblical truth, we will starve spiritually.

God is also against prophets who "steal [His] words from each other" (Jeremiah 23:30). Notice they are God's words, but false prophets have stolen them from others and share them as though God has given the words to them. That's called plagiarism.

In addition, God is against prophets "who use their tongues and declare, 'The Lord declares'" (Jeremiah 23:31). This is tragically happening in some churches. Several years ago, a pulpit committee stopped by my office for advice. The grandson of the former pastor had called the church and told them that God had revealed to him that he was to be the new pastor. Some on the committee believed that the message the grandson received was from God, but others were doubtful. If God had spoken to this man, they had better extend him an invitation, or they would be disobeying God. I asked what the young man was like. They said he seemed legitimate, but he lacked any formal education. They were also troubled by his request for absolute authority to carry out the plan God had given him for the church. He didn't want to work through the elders. I asked, "Don't you think God would work through the committee that was chosen by the congregation?"

Using God's name to persuade others is a ploy that God detests. I have counseled many who have been led astray because they have complied with other people's wishes who said they had heard from God. One young lady married a man because God told him they were to get married. She didn't want to disobey God. Pulling spiritual rank is spiritual abuse. Those who use God's name to get leverage for what they want can only expect disaster down the road.

Finally, God says, "Behold, I am against those who have prophesied false dreams," declares the Lord, "and reported them and led My people astray by their lies and reckless boasting;" (Jeremiah 23:32). They proclaim, "God is going to do a great work, a mighty work," or worse, "a new thing!" Such spiritual hype is not of God.

The purpose of the gift of prophecy is to turn people's hearts back to God according to 1 Corinthians 14:24,25:

> But if all prophesy, and an unbeliever or an ungifted man enters, he is convicted by all, he is called to account by all; the secrets of his heart are disclosed; and so, he will fall on his face and worship God, declaring that God is certainly among you.

God's Word is like fire; it purifies the church: "For it is time for judgment to begin with the household of God" (1 Peter 4:17). God is far more concerned about church purity than church growth because church purity is an essential prerequisite for church growth. Only the pure church can grow and bear fruit. Satan will use signs and wonders to lead people off the path of sanctification. He will divert our interest away from the eternal to the temporal and will appeal to the lusts of the flesh, the lust of the eyes, and the boastful pride of life. God's Word is like a hammer that breaks up the hard ground and softens the heart. If church people were living in immorality, and a word of prophecy came from the Lord, rest assured it would not be some generic word of comfort like, "Hang on I'm coming soon." It would reveal unrighteousness for the purpose of cleansing. That is what God's Word does. It cleanses the soul and draws us closer to Him in righteousness.

A Church Father said, "Test the man who says he is inspired – by his deeds and his life[18] (Hermas [c. 150]). You will know God's disciples by their love and humility. The warnings against false prophets are numerous in the New Testament:

> Beloved, do not believe every spirit, but test the spirits to see whether they are from God; because many false prophets have gone out into the world (1 John 4:1).

> And many false prophets will arise and will mislead many... for false Christs and false prophets will arise and will show great signs and wonders, so as to mislead, if possible, even the elect (Matthew 24:11,24).

Beware of false prophets, who come to you in sheep's clothing, but inwardly are ravenous wolves. You will know them by their fruits... Not everyone who says to me, "Lord, Lord," will enter the kingdom of heaven, but he who does the will of my Father, who is in heaven will enter. Many will say to me on that day, "Lord, Lord, did we not prophesy in your name, and in your name cast out demons, and in your name perform many miracles?"

They may prophesy, cast out demons and even perform miracles in the name of the Lord. And then I will declare to them, "I never knew you; Depart from me, you who practice lawlessness" (Matthew 7:15,16,19-23).

For such men are false apostles, deceitful workers, disguising themselves as apostles of Christ. And no wonder, for even Satan disguises himself as an angel of light. Therefore, it is not surprising if his servants also disguise themselves as servants of righteousness; whose end shall be according to their deeds (2 Corinthians 11:13-15).

False religions and cults can be identified by their doctrines, which they make no attempt to hide. That is not the case for false prophets and teachers who identify themselves as Christians and work within the church:

> But false prophets also arose among the people, just as there will also be false teachers among you, who will secretly introduce destructive heresies, even denying the Master who bought them, bringing swift destruction upon themselves. And many will follow their sensuality, and because of them the way of the truth will be maligned; and in their greed, they will exploit you with false words; their judgment from long ago is not idle, and their destruction is not asleep (2 Peter 2:1-3).

False teachers disguise themselves as ministers of righteousness. What we see seldom threatens the church. External and visible opposition can have a purging effect on the church that leaves the body stronger. False teachers are infiltrators whose purpose is to influence the church in a covert, negative way. These "tares are the sons of the evil one; and the enemy who sowed them is the devil" (Matthew 13:38). Their purpose is to secretly introduce destructive heresies. A heretic is someone who causes schisms. If we were spiritually alert, we would, "reject a factious man after a first and second warning" (Titus 3:10). Heretics seek to discredit righteous workers and sow disunity. They seduce people through their "sensuality." The result is that many people will be mesmerized and follow their destructive ways.

Another characteristic of false prophets and teachers is their rebellious heart. They despise authority (2 Peter 2:10). This may be the easiest way to spot them. They won't answer to anyone. They have independent spirits and are not compatible with those who desire to live righteously. True Christian leaders have a servant's heart and don't seek to lord it over others. They prove to be an example (see 1 Peter 5:1-4). True leaders don't appeal to their title or position to enhance their status or demand allegiance (see Matthew 20:20-28). The only identity and position they need is the one every believer already has in Christ. The authoritative teaching of a true leader rests upon their godly character and is based on their position in Christ, not on some title bestowed upon them by themselves or others. What title did Jesus have other than the Son of God? "When Jesus had finished these words, the crowds were amazed at his teaching; for He was teaching them as one having authority, and not as their scribes" (Matthew 7:28,29). Being children of God is the only title we need.

As you guard yourself against false prophets, I caution you not to go on a witch-hunt. Some heresy hunters are self-righteous, arrogant, and judgmental. They become as divisive as the heretics they try to expose. We can't focus on what is wrong for too long, because it will have a negative effect on ourselves. We should be known for what we believe, not for what we don't believe. Knowing the truth exposes the lies, but knowing the lies doesn't reveal the truth. Good people can be deceived, and we should show them the light, not the exit.

The name it and claim it "prophets" sound more like New Age practitioners than gospel preachers. They deceptively say, "If you can conceive it, you can achieve it," or "It will become true if you believe hard enough." We don't create reality with our minds. God's Word is true; therefore, we believe it. Believing God's Word does not make it true, and not believing it doesn't make it false. We are mentally healthy when we are in touch with reality, and the ultimate reality is God.

A few years ago, I received a letter from the senior pastor of an Assemblies of God Church in Singapore. One of his staff wanted to take a group of people to Ephesus where Christian intercessors were going to gather and "pray out the queen of heaven." The rationale for such an event was based on a paper by one who presented himself as a prophet. He taught that the apostle Paul had gone to Ephesus and defeated the goddess Diana. I responded by asking the pastor a question: Did the Apostle Paul defeat the goddess Diana, or did Jesus disarm Satan at the cross and Paul went to Ephesus preaching the full gospel, which the people believed and repented of their worship of false gods and idols? He was thankful and said, "We're not going," which was a wise choice, because the event amounted to nothing.

The humility of that pastor was impressive. He was twenty years older than I was, and age is venerated in Asia He was also the head of the Pentecostal church in that area. After I preached the Sunday morning after the conference, he closed by saying, "I have learned a lot this week. I don't have to shout out to the devil. I can simply take my place in Christ and help these people repent."

Authority and Power

Jesus had already demonstrated His superiority over the natural and spiritual realms when He "called the twelve together, and gave them power and authority over all the demons and to heal diseases" (Luke 9:1), and sent them out to proclaim the kingdom of God. Power is the ability to rule, and authority is the right to rule over the kingdom of darkness.

Then Jesus appointed seventy others and sent them out. "The seventy returned with joy, saying, 'Lord, even the demons are subject to us in Your name'" (Luke 10:17). At that time, it would take some uniquely endowed authority agent to triumph over the demonic realm, which was limited to Jesus, the twelve disciples, and the seventy others. Who has the right to rule is the issue in spiritual warfare, and that is what Jesus settled forever when He came to undo the works of Satan. Having completed His work, Jesus said, "All authority has been given to Me in heaven and on earth. Go therefore and make disciples of all the nations" (Matthew 28:18,19).

The disciples were told to wait in Jerusalem until they received power when the Holy Spirit came upon them (Acts 1:3,8). Everything changed after Pentecost, which marked the beginning of the Church under the New Covenant. That is why there are no instructions in the epistles to cast out demons. Satan is disarmed and God's children are seated with Christ in the heavenlies. Every child of God has the same power and authority that the disciples were given. Paul instructs the Church how to set captives free and heal the wounded in 2 Timothy 2:24-26:

> The Lord's bond-servant must not be quarrelsome, but be kind to all, able to teach, patient when wronged, with gentleness correcting those who are in opposition, if perhaps God may grant them repentance leading to the knowledge of the truth, and they may come to their senses and escape from the snare of the devil, having been held captive by him to do his will.

Truth Encounter

That is not a power encounter as commonly perceived. It is a truth encounter that requires the Lord's bond-servant to be totally dependent upon God. True disciples are kind, patient, gentle, and able to teach. It is because of their position in Christ that they have the authority to do God's will. They have no spiritual authority to work independently of God. Bond-servants of Jesus are authoritative, not authoritarian like false apostles and prophets. Paul sets the example in 1 Corinthians 2:4-7:

> Just as we have been approved by God to be entrusted with the gospel, so we speak, not as pleasing men, but God who examines our hearts. For we never came with flattering speech, as you know, nor with a pretext for greed – God is witness – nor did we seek glory from men, either from you or from others, even though as apostles of Christ we might have asserted our authority. But we proved to be gentle among you, as a nursing mother tenderly cares for her own children.

We also have the power to rule over the kingdom of darkness provided we walk according to the Spirit, but don't if we live according to the flesh:

> I pray that the eyes of your heart may be enlightened, so that you will know...what is the surpassing greatness of His power toward us who believe. These are in accordance with the working of the strength of His might which He brought about in Christ, when He raised Him from the dead and seated Him at His right hand in the heavenly places, far

above all rule and authority and power and dominion, and every name that is named, not only in this age but also in the one to come (Ephesians 1:16-20).

The Bible gives no instruction to seek more power, because we already have all the power, we need to do God's will. Seeking something we already have, and trying to become somebody we already are can only lead to error. Our hearts need to be enlightened so we can know the riches that have already been extended to us who believe and take our place in Christ.

It is not our role to defeat the devil. He has already been disarmed and judged (John 6:11). It is not our role to assume responsibility for those we are trying to help. The lives of struggling people are like a house where the garbage hasn't been taken out in months. That will attract a lot of flies. Trying to ascertain the names of the flies and determining their rank is not the answer. Getting rid of the garbage is the answer. Repentance and faith in God are and always will be the answer in this present church age. You can't put on the armor of God for another person, but you can teach them how they can. You can't submit to God and resist the devil for them (James 4:7), but you can help them do it, which is what Paul instructed us to do. Christ is the deliverer, we're not. If you sense that a person's problem is demonic, it might seem easier to cast a demon out of them, but what is to prevent the demon from coming back, and bringing seven more (see Matthew 12:45)?

Effective ministries help others assume responsibility for their own health and well-being. We cannot live an irresponsible life and expect God to heal us and set us free. So, what should people do if they are suffering according to James?

Is anyone among you suffering? Then he must pray. Is anyone cheerful: He is to sing praises. Is anyone among you sick? Then he must call for the elders of the church and they are to pray over him, anointing him with oil in the name of the Lord; and the prayer offered in faith will restore the one who is sick, and the Lord will raise him up, and if he has committed sins, they will be forgiven him. Therefore, confess your sins to one another so that you may be healed. The effective prayer of a righteous man can accomplish much (James 5: 13-16).

If the person who is suffering is willing to pray themselves, assume responsibility for their own health, take the initiative by asking for help, and confess their sins, then the prayer of a righteous person will accomplish much. I have seen incredible answers to prayer after we have helped people resolve their personal and spiritual conflicts through genuine repentance and faith in God.

Suppose a man calls your church and asks for the elders to pray for him. Let's say that the elders are godly men who agree to fast for a day before the time of prayer. They have done their part, but what if the man who is asking for prayer is in the bondage of bitterness along with a host of other issues keeping him from having an intimate relationship with his Heavenly Father? Do you expect God to answer his plea for healing? I don't. I would have him repent and believe the gospel and then pray. Those who may have the gift of healing will be a lot more effective if they help the person live a righteous life. The same follows for those who have any spiritual gift. They will accomplish more if they and their workers are living righteous lives.

It is required of us to be good stewards of all that God has entrusted to us (1 Corinthians 4:1,2). There is a health benefit for those who live a righteous life and have a proper balance of rest, exercise, and diet. When God calls such saints home, they don't cry and wail demanding God to heal them. They die with dignity and without fear, which impresses the medical field far more than occasional healing.

God wants His children to prosper. "Beloved, I pray that in all respects you may prosper and be in good health, just as your soul prospers" (2 John 2). However, what is your definition of prosperity? Those who peddle the "prosperity gospel" are the ones who usually end up with most of the money (your money), and they pay little attention to restoring the soul. God wants our souls to prosper, and when you "seek first His kingdom and His righteousness" (Matthew 6: 33) all the things you need will be added to you.

Therefore, "Delight yourself in the Lord; and He will give you the desires of your heart" (Psalm 37:4). What do you think would happen if you first delighted yourself in the Lord? Your desires would change. If you don't first delight yourself in the Lord, then your desires will be of the flesh, and the flesh cannot be satisfied. But if you delight yourself in the Lord, your desires will be for love, joy, peace, patience, kindness, goodness, faithfulness, gentleness, and self-control. What would you exchange for the fruit of the Spirit? A new car? A bigger house? "But those who want to get rich fall into temptation and a snare and many foolish and harmful desires which plunge men into ruin and destruction. For the love of money is a root of all sorts of evil" (1 Timothy 6:9,10). Delighting yourself in the Lord will give you what you really desire and nobody and nothing can keep you from having it. "For I am convinced that neither death, nor life, nor angels, nor principalities, nor things present, nor things to come, nor powers, nor height, nor depth, nor any other created thing, will be able to separate us from the love of God, which is in Christ Jesus our Lord" (Romans 8:38,39).

Discussion Questions

1. What is the foundation for our faith and who laid that foundation?
2. What is the primary purpose of the gift of prophecy?
3. How can we identify false prophets, teachers, and Messiahs?
4. What is the difference between authority and power, and what qualifies the believer to possess both?
5. How has the New Covenant, which was inaugurated at Pentecost, changed how believers overcome the kingdom of darkness?
6. According to 2 Timothy 2:24-26, what qualifies a believer to set captives free and what must the captive do?
7. What are the limits and scope of the believer's authority over the kingdom of darkness?
8. Why should we get rid of the garbage before we chase off the flies?
9. What is your definition of prosperity?
10. Why must we first delight ourselves in the Lord, and what will happen if we do?

Chapter Five: Overcoming Spiritism

It appears probable enough that this man [Marcus, a heretic] possesses a demon as a familiar spirit. By means of this spirit, he seems to be able to prophesy. He also enables others to prophesy – as many as he counts worthy to be partakers of his charis... However, the gift of prophecy is not conferred on men by Marcus, the magician. Rather, only those to whom God sends His grace from above possess the divinely bestowed power of prophesying. And they speak where and when God wishes, not when Marcus orders them to do so.[19]

Irenaeus (c. 180)

There were prophets a very long time ago more ancient than these who are reputed to be philosophers, blessed and righteous and dear to God. They spoke by a divine Spirit, and they oracularly predicted future events which are now taking place. They are truly called prophets... Past events and events now taking place compel us to agree with what was spoken by them. Furthermore, they deserved to be believed because of the miracles which they performed, since they were glorifying God the Creator and Father of the universe and they were announcing the Christ coming from Him, His Son. The false prophets who were filled with the deceitful and filthy spirit never did nor now do this. They dare to work various supposed miracles to impress men, and they glorify the spirits and demons of deceit.[20]

Justin Martyr, "Dialogue with Trypho"

Signs and Wonders

The late John Wimber was an adjunct professor at Fuller Seminary and co-taught a class on signs and wonders. He was the founder of the Vineyard movement and wrote two popular books entitled *Power Evangelism* and *Power Healing*. John began his ministry as an evangelical and later became a leader in the charismatic movement.

We were both making presentations at a conference, and I mentioned to him in a private conversation my appreciation for his two books, but I had a couple of questions that I hoped he would help me with. First, I thought it was one thing for him to move into a greater understanding of the Holy Spirit's work, and another thing for young converts who were not as theologically grounded as he was. John responded by saying, "That is the biggest problem in our movement. Everybody wants the power, but not enough want to study God's Word and become disciplined in their spiritual walk."

Second, in the New Testament every time the words signs, and wonders occur, either by themselves or together, they are attributed to a false teacher, false prophet, or false messiah when the context refers to end times. I asked John if he was aware of that. He was surprised, but sobered as well, and invited me to speak at their annual Vineyard convention, which I did.

God has made His presence known through signs and wonders, as He did in the early church: "Everyone kept feeling a sense of awe; and many wonders and signs were taking place through the apostles" (Acts 2:43). However, we have an obligation to teach that the devil is a counterfeiter and will also make use of signs and wonders to lead us astray. "Beloved, do not believe every spirit, but test the spirits to see whether they are from God, because many false prophets have gone out into the world" (1 John 4:1). In these deceptive times we must have our "senses trained to discern good and evil" (Hebrews 5:14, see chapter 5 on spiritual discernment).

Spiritism is the dominant religious orientation in the world. It is the worldview of the native population of the Americas, and of every primitive culture. There is no formal structure to spiritism, but spiritists believe there are spiritual forces that affect how they live. Appeasing these deities, or trying to manipulate them, is part of their daily ritual. Most believe there is a supreme – but unapproachable – spirit.

Most Americans are not likely to participate in Native American worship, but many do participate in occultic practices and are mentally oppressed as a result. Change the name from 'medium' to 'psychic', and 'demon' to 'spirit guide', and a gullible public sees no harm. Psychics and New Age practitioners believe that Jesus was the ultimate psychic, because He could read people's minds. They believe spirit guides were enlightening Jesus. When Jesus revealed what Jewish leaders were thinking, they too proclaimed, "You have a demon" (John 7:20). The Jewish community at the time of Christ was aware that such esoteric knowledge had to come from some supernatural source. Knowing whether you are paying attention to a deceiving spirit or being led by the Holy Spirit has been a major challenge throughout Church history.

The first issue we attempt to resolve in *The Steps to Freedom in Christ* is counterfeit guidance, i.e., they renounce any involvement in a cult or occultic practices. Paul said, "we have renounced the things hidden because of shame, not walking in craftiness or adulterating the word of God" (2 Corinthians 2:2). This is what the early church did when they faced the West and said, "I renounce you Satan, and all your works, and all your ways." Then they would face the East and make their profession of faith in Christ. Roman Catholic and Eastern Orthodox converts still make that declaration when being confirmed.

The Seduction of Our Children

Many issues that adults struggle with originated when they were young and vulnerable. The average adult will check off ten occultic experiences when they process *The Steps*. To find out what was going on with teenagers, we conducted research in preparation for our book, *The Seduction of Our Children*.[21] In one conservative Christian high school forty-five percent said they had experienced a "presence" (seen or heard) in their room that scared them. Fifty-five percent said they had harbored bad thoughts about God. Forty-five percent said they found it mentally hard to pray and read their Bibles. Sixty-nine percent reported hearing "voices" in their heads, like there was a subconscious voice talking to them. Twenty-two percent said they frequently entertained suicide thoughts. Seventy-four percent said they were different from others, i.e., 'Christianity works for others, but not for me'. Of course, that is not true, but if they believe that they will live accordingly.

We found a direct correlation between those percentages and their involvement with occultic experiences such as astral projection, table lifting, fortune telling, astrology, Dungeons and Dragons, crystals and pyramids, Ouija boards, automatic writing, tarot cards, palm reading, spirit guides, and blood pacts. That research was conducted before smartphones. The publisher asked if we would like to do a second edition with current research, but we struggled to find churches or schools that would permit it.

The Lure of Knowledge and Power

The lure of knowledge and power has trapped many in Satan's web. To illustrate, I received the following email from a former psychic:

> I just finished your DVD based on The Bondage Breaker, in which you discuss deception and the lure of knowledge and power. As a former channeler, let me share how psychics work. They only know what they are told by demons, and demons only know that which they have observed or what has been spoken out. For example, if my husband and I were talking about going to Hawaii for a vacation and I went to see a psychic, they might say something like, "I see you on vacation somewhere warm. There is a beach and sand. You're with a tall dark man – your husband. I believe it is Hawaii.

Of course, anyone would be impressed (deceived) by that apparent knowledge of the unknown. I worked as a psychic and ran in circles with those who were very "gifted" in that area. I got hooked at an early age. They were always able to tell me what had been spoken out and even some things that looked like they might happen. For example, I have always been a writer (and musician) and they would tell me that I was talented and would succeed in both areas, but everyone (even non-channelers) told me that because of my passion for writing. It was an obvious gift, and I was persistent. So of course, I would naturally find ways to get published and eventually that happened. It did not happen in the time-frame they predicted, because that was unknown to them – so they bluffed their way through. Some of their future predictions happened and some of them didn't. What I did notice was that a psychic could give intimate details about a person's past, but not their future. That was always vague and often untrue in the unfolding events.

The key to becoming a good psychic is submitting to "the spirit," which I was constantly told. I had the "gift," but it would be stronger/better if I'd only submit more. I was told I was rebelling from my "gift" when I resisted. God is gracious and merciful. There was always something (the Lord no doubt) that held me back from fully committing, and even though I was not a believer I eventually saw the inconsistency and deception, and slowly stepped away. After becoming a believer and going through your *Steps to Freedom in Christ* I was set free from my involvement in these areas and saw the entire deception clearly.

A pastor friend of mine received a letter from a former staff member who was dismissed for moral reasons but who was now pastoring a church he had planted in the same community. The letter contained a prophecy for my friend's church. I asked, "Why would God give a prophetic message to your church through the pastor of another church?" I suggested that they shouldn't listen to it since it would function like a curse. From the time they read it, everything that happened in the church would be evaluated by the prophecy (either to substantiate or invalidate it). The false prophecy had taken precedence over the leading of the Holy Spirit. I recommended that he call Jack Hayford who gave him the same advice. <u>God will always work through the lines of authority that He has established in His Word</u>.

Guidelines For Using the Gift of Prophesy

The Apostle Paul wrote, "Do not quench the Spirit; do not despise prophetic utterances but examine everything carefully; hold fast to that which is good; abstain from every form of evil" (1 Thessalonians 5:19-21). To examine carefully I offer the following tests and guidelines:

First, is the person giving the prophetic utterance living a balanced and righteous life?

Second, are they committed to building God's kingdom or are they enhancing their own status, i.e., is Christ being exalted or are they being exalted?

Third, is the prophetic utterance in agreement with God's Word? The Holy Spirit will never contradict His Word. Prophetic utterances are no substitute for God's Word. Saying whatever comes to your mind may seem a lot easier than being "diligent to present yourself approved to God as a workman who does not need to be ashamed, accurately handling the word of truth" (2 Timothy 2:15). Christian maturity and learning to speak the truth in love are not matters of expediency.

Fourth, does the use of a spiritual gift bring unity to the church and edify others? Be careful in this test, because those who hold to a form of godliness but deny its power are not in balance either. They will quench the Spirit through censorship and very little will be accomplished in the church.

Fifth, do the spiritual manifestations bypass the mind? God speaks to and through minds that are fully engaged. "I will pray with the Spirit, and I will pray with the mind also; I will sing with the Spirit, and I will sing with the mind also" (1 Corinthians 14:15). If a person takes on a medium-like trance, be assured it is occultic. God renews our minds and brings back to our minds all that He has taught us. He can only do that if we have first put into our minds the Word of God.

A seminary student told me that he was having difficulty getting to school on time. What should have been a five-minute drive lengthened to forty-five minutes, because a voice in his mind kept telling him to turn at intersections. Not wanting to disobey what he perceived to be the "still small quiet voice of God," he was treated to a tour of the city almost every morning. A pastor's wife passively believed that whatever entered her mind was from God. She soon found herself bound by fear and plagued by condemning thoughts. John Wesley wrote:

> Do not hastily ascribe things to God. Do not easily suppose dreams, voices, impressions, visions, or revelations to be from God. They may be from Him. They may be from nature. They may be from the devil. Therefore, do not believe every spirit, but try the spirits, whether they are from God.[22]

Martin Wells Knapp, co-founder of the Wesleyan Church, wrote the book *Impressions: From God or Satan, How to Know the Difference*.[23] Writing at the end of the 19th century, Knapp makes a distinction between the lies of Satan and the leading of the Holy Spirit:

> There are the voices of evil and deceiving spirits who lie in wait to entrap every traveler entering the higher regions of spiritual life. In the same epistle that tells us we are seated in heavenly places in Christ, we are also told that we will have to fight with spiritual enemies. These spiritual enemies, whoever or whatever they may be, must necessarily communicate with us by means of our spiritual faculties. And their voices, as the voice of God, are an inward impression made upon our spirit. Therefore, just as the Holy Spirit may tell us by impressions what the will of God is concerning us, so also will these spiritual enemies tell us by impression what is their will concerning us, though not of course giving it their name.[24]

In the same book, Knapp wrote,

> Oh, that I could write one message with the point of a diamond upon the heart of every Christian. It should be this: Be sure that the slightest impression upon your heart disposing you to do Christian work has a divine stamp. And then obey it at whatever cost.

Think As to Have Sound Judgment

It is our responsibility to actively use our minds to know and choose to believe the truth. Inducing a passive state of mind through drugs or self-hypnosis or becoming morbidly introspective is the most dangerous thing that we can do spiritually. As we have noted, God never bypasses our minds. He works through them. We are transformed by the renewing of our minds (Romans 12:2). We are, "to think so as to have sound judgment" (Romans 12:3). "Brethren, do not be children in your thinking; yet in evil be babes, but in your thinking be mature" (1 Corinthians 14:20). We must also gird up our minds for action (1 Peter 1:13). That means that we don't play fantasy games or use visualization techniques that are not based on truth. Nor do we live in an imaginary world. It is okay and helpful to visualize yourself doing something as long as you do it and it is consistent with God's Word. That is how we gird up our minds for action.

The mind is to be fully engaged when exercising every gift of God. Counterfeit gifts will bypass our minds. A young man was heralded as a prophet and was invited to several churches, but when he came to see me, he was under psychiatric care. I asked him when he first received his prophetic gift and it happened when he was coached by others to speak in tongues. Scripture tells us to test the spirit, not the person. So, I asked him to speak in tongues thus manifesting the spirit and asked the spirit to identify itself. A voice said, "I am he." I said, "Are you the Christ, the Son of the living God?" His head shook and with a gravelly voice said, "No, not he!" Wrong spirit! It is not our role to distribute spiritual gifts. "But one and the same Spirit works all these things, distributing to each one individually just as he wills" (1 Corinthians 12:11).

Taking Every Thought Captive

Paul's message to the church at Corinth specifically addressed their immorality and misuse of spiritual gifts. He advised them to assume responsibility for what they are thinking. "We are destroying speculations and every lofty thing raised up against the knowledge of God, and we are taking every thought (*noema*) captive to the obedience of Christ" (2 Corinthians 10:5). The word noema only occurs six times in scripture (five times in 2 Corinthians) and the context reveals the possible origin of those "thoughts."

The first occurrence is in 2 Corinthians 2:10,11, "But whom you forgive anything, I forgive also; for indeed what I have forgiven, if I have forgiven anything, I did it for your sakes in the presence of Christ in order that no advantage be taken of us by Satan; for we are not ignorant of his schemes" (*noema*). Forgiving others as Christ has forgiven us is the most Christlike thing we can do. Satan will take advantage of our unforgiveness and keep us bound to our past. "See to it that no one comes short of the grace of God; that no root of bitterness springing up causes trouble, and by it, many be defiled" (Hebrews 12:15).

The second and third occurrence of *noema* is 2 Corinthians 3:14; 4:3,4:

> But their minds (*noema*) were hardened; for until this very day at the reading of the Old Covenant, the same veil remains unlifted, because it is removed in Christ ... And even if our gospel is veiled, it is veiled to those who are perishing, in whose case the god of this world has blinded the minds (noema) of the unbelieving, that they might not see the light of the gospel of the glory of Christ, who is the image of God.

The last occurrence of *noema* in 2 Corinthians is 11:3,4, "But I am afraid, lest as the serpent deceived Eve by his craftiness, your minds (noema) should be led astray from the simplicity and purity of devotion to Christ. For if one comes and preaches another Jesus whom we have not preached, or you receive a different spirit which you have not received or a different gospel which you have not accepted, you bear this beautifully." What cults teach about Jesus is heretical and leads to a gospel of works aided by an evil spirit.

Other than 2 Corinthians, the only other place *noema* is used is Philippians 4:7, "The peace of God, which surpasses all comprehension, will guard your hearts and your minds (noema) in Christ Jesus." It is our responsibility to take every thought (*noema*) captive to the obedience of Christ. If what we are thinking isn't true, then don't believe it. We don't win this battle by rebuking negative thoughts; we win the battle by choosing the truth. Remember, we are not called to dispel the darkness; we are called to turn on the light. Paul instructs us how in Philippians 4:8,9:

> Finally, brethren, whatever is true, whatever is honorable, whatever is right, whatever is pure, whatever is lovely, whatever is of good repute, if there is any excellence and if anything is worthy of praise, let your mind dwell on those things. The things you have learned and received and heard and seen in me, practice these things; and the God of peace shall be with you.

Inner Healing

Many inner healing ministries have become popular around the world, and they vary considerably in theory and practice. The idea is to invite Jesus to take inquirers back to earlier experiences in their lives to root out embedded lies and replace them with truth. People are indeed living in bondage to lies such as, "I'm no good, God doesn't love me, it's all my fault," which they have believed because of past traumas. Under the guidance of a mature and discerning facilitator who can sense when the wrong "Jesus" shows up (which does happen), it can be a meaningful experience.

However, replacing an embedded lie with the truth is just one part of a much larger repentance process. There are many other critical issues that surface when people go through *The Steps* like renouncing counterfeit guidance, overcoming deception, pride, rebellion, sexual sins, and unforgiveness. To overcome personal and spiritual conflicts other questions need to be asked. Does the person know who they are in Christ? Do they understand their position in Christ and the authority they have over the enemy? Have they repented from all their other sins and forgiven those who have offended them? Do they understand the battle that is going on for their mind and know why they need to take every thought captive to the obedience of Christ? Genuine repentance and faith in God accomplish inner healing and far more. The results are longer lasting because inquirers have assumed their responsibility to resolve personal and spiritual conflicts.

God has gifted His children, and the Holy Spirit manifests His presence in our lives. There have been occasions when God has given me "the word of knowledge," which is a manifestation of the Holy Spirit (1 Corinthians 12:8), but it should be tested like any other manifestation. Suppose while helping an individual I sense that the person is struggling with homosexuality. I would test that by asking a probing question at the proper time like, "Have you ever struggled with homosexual thoughts or tendencies?" This accomplishes three goals. First, if that impression wasn't from God, they would simply say no. In the process, I haven't falsely accused them of anything, and it does no damage to the relationship.

Second, if they are struggling with homosexual issues, I am giving them an opportunity to share that without condemnation. In my experience that is usually what happens.

Third, if they are struggling with those issues, but don't want to share them with me at that time, I respect that choice.

Corporate Repentance

Churches, like people, need to be set free from spiritual bondages as well. Repentance is not only an individual responsibility, but also a corporate responsibility that leaders will be held accountable for. The writer of Hebrews said that you should "Obey your leaders and submit to them, for they keep watch over your souls as those who will give an account" (Hebrews 13:17). The elders are the spiritual leaders of the church and have the responsibility for the spiritual condition of the church. Charles Mylander and I wrote a book entitled *Setting Your Church Free*[25] that explains a corporate repentance process based on the seven churches in Revelation. *The Steps to Setting Your Church Free* process is similar to the individual *The Steps* in that both are dependent upon the presence and leading of God. Jesus is not only the Wonderful Counselor, but He is also the ultimate church consultant. The word "I" occurs fifty times in the messages to the seven churches. "I" is the Lord Jesus, the head of the Church, and He is calling them to repentance. Every message to the seven churches ends with the same statement: "He who has an ear, let him hear what the Spirit says to the churches."

Most readers are probably aware of the church in Ephesus that lost its first love, or the church of Laodicea that is lukewarm. What is often overlooked is how many struggled with demonic strongholds.

> To Smyrna: "I know the slander of those who say they are Jews and are not but are *a synagogue of Satan*. Do not be afraid of what you are about to suffer. I tell you; *the devil* will put some of you in prison to test you, and you will suffer persecution for ten days (Revelation 2:9-10, emphasis added).

What people saw were Jews who slandered the Christians in Smyrna. What Jesus saw was a "synagogue of Satan." What people saw were Roman rulers who threw Christians into jail. What Jesus saw was the devil who put some of them in prison. Not all synagogues were demonized, but this one was. The enemies of the gospel were doing the devil's work by attacking the church in Smyrna.

> To Pergamum: "I know where you live – where Satan has his throne. Yet you remain true to my name. You did not renounce your faith in me, even in the days of Antipas, my faithful witness, who was put to death in your city – *where Satan lives* (Revelation 2:13, emphasis added)

What people saw was a city on a hill with major temples upon it. What Jesus saw was Satan's throne. What people saw was the center of emperor worship in Asia. The place was oppressive to Christians, killing some and threatening others.

> To Thyatira: "Now I say to the rest of you in Thyatira, to you who do not hold to her teaching and have not learned *Satan's so-called deep secrets* (I will not impose any other burden on you): Only hold on to what you have until I come" (Revelation 2:24,25, emphasis added).

What people saw was a prophetess who taught that, since grace covered every sin, it was okay to indulge in the pagan temple feasts. What Jesus saw was Satan's deceptive secrets for indulging in sexual sins and satanic rituals

> To Philadelphia: "I will make those who are of the *synagogue of Satan*, who claim to be Jews though they are not, but are liars – I will make them come and fall down at your feet and acknowledge that I have loved you" (Revelation 3:9, emphasis added).

What people saw was a divided fellowship. What Jesus saw was a demonized synagogue and He was about to prove His love for the faithful. It has been my privilege to lead the leaders of a denomination, a seminary, para-church ministries, and several churches through *The Steps to Setting Your Church Free*. Some individuals dragged their feet coming in, but not going out, because they heard from God. Those who asked for the process were good ministries that wanted to be better. Heavily conflicted churches are almost always in bad shape because of the leadership, and they won't submit to the process because it would expose them. The best time to process corporate repentance is when they leave. One of our staff ministered to the following church:

I purchased a set of Neil's CDs on "Resolving Personal and Spiritual Conflicts." I began applying his principles and started to realize that many of my difficulties were spiritual attacks. I learned how to take a stand and won victories over some of my problems.

That was only the tip of the iceberg. I'm a deacon and preacher in a Baptist church. My pastor was suffering from depression and other problems that I was not aware of, and then he committed suicide. That brought our church to its knees. I knew some of the problems of previous pastors and believed they were spiritual, but I didn't know how to relay it to the congregation since we had been taught that a demon cannot affect a Christian!

The church elected me as their interim pastor. In a bookstore, I came across Neil's book entitled *Setting Your Church Free*. I purchased it and read it. With all the spiritual suppression in our church I believed that was the answer, but how do I get the rest of the church to believe? The pastor who committed suicide would not read or listen to your message. Slowly the people accepted my message, and I contacted one of your staff and he led our leaders through *"The Steps to Setting Your Church Free."* The leaders loved it. Next, I wanted to take all the people through *The Steps to Freedom in Christ*. Six weeks later, I was able to do so. I really don't understand it, but we were set free from the spiritual bondage of multiple problems. I can't put it in a letter, or I would write a book.

During all this time, one of my middle-aged members, an evangelist, was set free. He learned who he was in Christ and is back in ministry. I saw the daughters of the deceased pastor set free, and forgive their father, and they were able to get on with their lives. One of the girls was contemplating suicide.

This is a new church; God is free to work here. When you do things God's way, you get God's results. I also work one night a week in our county jail, which is the second largest in the country. I work with homosexual men, and I have seen many set free.

Discussion Questions

1. Why should we be cautious about signs and wonders?
2. How can parents prepare their children to stand firm in Christ against the devil's schemes?
3. How do psychics lure us away with false prophecies and esoteric knowledge?
4. What are the guidelines for properly using the gift of prophecy?
5. Why is it so important for believers to take every thought captive to the obedience of Christ?
6. How can believers win the battle for their minds?
7. How can believers experience inner healing?
8. Who is responsible for corporate repentance?
9. What do the seven letters to the seven churches in Revelation reveal about the struggles that churches have?
10. What is your personal takeaway from this chapter?

Chapter Six: Overcoming Satanism

From this, we learn that this was the apostate angel and the enemy. For he was envious of God's workmanship and took in hand to render this workmanship into something at enmity with God. For this reason, too, God has banished from His presence the one who of his own accord stealthily sowed the tares. I am referring to the one who brought about the transgression.[26]

Irenaeus (c. 180)

God made another being, in whom the disposition of the divine origin did not remain. Therefore, he was infected with his own envy, as with poison. So, he passed from good to evil. Through his own will, which had been given to him by God unfettered, he acquired for himself a name. We call him the *Accuser*, for he reports to God the faults to which he himself entices.[27]

Lactantius (c. 304)

An association of campus security directors was having its monthly meeting and our director asked me to speak to them about Satanism. I was surprised that he asked, since this wasn't a Christian association and I had never before spoken, even to a Christian group on that subject. Ten minutes into my talk their hands began to rise, and I was the one who needed to be educated. Every director in attendance regularly found sacrificial remains on their campus. All were told to keep it quiet by the administration. I was even more surprised to learn that our director had found the remains of ritual sacrifices on our Christian campus, and that was the reason he asked me to speak on Satanism.

Encountering Satanism

While teaching at Talbot School of Theology, and before I went public with my ministry, God gave me a crash course on the covert activities of Satanism. I wasn't looking for it, and I had never given any thought to the idea that there are people who actually worship Satan. It began when I received a phone call from a lady requesting help for a boarder. She was a backslidden Christian who rented part of her home to Harry, a man in his forties. Harry claimed to have been raised a Satanist, but now he wanted out of it. I arranged for the three of us to meet at our church on a Saturday afternoon. After hearing his story, I said, "You can't just leave Satanism and go nowhere, because you would still be in the kingdom of darkness. Are you prepared to make a decision for Christ?" Harry started to shake, and I could sense the oppression.

I didn't want to proceed without prayer support, and his nominal Christian lady friend wouldn't be much help for that. So, I asked them to wait while I looked to see who was available. The only other person on location was the custodian, who was a strong believer. I explained the situation and said to him, "You don't have to do anything, just be there to support me in prayer."

Back in my office, I asked Harry if he was ready to make a decision for Christ. When he said, "Yes," all hell broke loose. I had never seen anything like that before. Fortunately, I had already learned how to deal with demonic forces without losing control, so I didn't respond in fear, which is the enemy's intended goal. Fear of Satan and faith in God are mutually exclusive. I opened my Bible and started reading aloud from the first chapter of Ephesians. I inserted Harry's name as follows: "Blessed be the God and Father of our Lord Jesus Christ, who has blessed Harry in Christ with every spiritual blessing in heavenly places," etc. I continued through most of the chapter. Harry crumbled to the floor and was lying prostrate on his stomach. With a great deal of effort, he managed to say one word at a time, "Lord Jesus, I need you." Suddenly the weight was lifted from him, and the oppression in the room was gone.

That was the humblest decision for Christ that I had ever seen, but the struggle for freedom was just beginning. The mental harassment was intense, and Satanists were making threatening calls. He was physically attacked, hog-tied, and branded in his own home. Two Christian men volunteered to be with him wherever he went.

Students at the seminary asked me about signs and symbols of Satanism, and I only knew about goats' heads and pentagrams. So, I asked Harry what he could share with me, and the next time we met he showed me a page of symbols that supposedly related to the summoning and sending of demons. Most of the symbols were related to sexual deviancy. A second page had seals identifying the seven major covens of the world. Two of the seven seals were designated for the Eastern and Western United States. I had no idea if what he was showing me was true or not, and there was no way to verify it one way or another. However, I did see the seal designated for the western United States etched into the skin of three unrelated individuals. Harry's landlord called to say that Harry had made a deal with Satanists. They would stop their harassment if he stopped sharing his testimony. You don't make deals with the devil, and that was the last I heard of Harry.

Clueless Counselors

A local counselor asked if I could sit in with a client to assess if there was anything spiritual going on with his client. He told me he didn't really believe in the demonic and asking me was a last resort. Four years of counseling and a battery of psychological and physical exams had resulted in nothing. If that counselor couldn't see the enemy's tactics in this young lady, he would never see it. She was waking up in the morning with cuts on her body and had no idea how they were getting there. She was switching personalities at night and attending satanic rituals from midnight to three in the morning. She wore long-sleeved shirts to cover the scars.

Some of her scars looked similar to the ones Harry showed me. When I pulled out the sheet to compare, she suddenly shrieked when she accidentally saw the symbol for western United States. I asked, "Where have you seen that?" "Right here," she said, as she pointed to her chest. On a subsequent visit, I asked if there were any more cuts, and she said yes. Pulling up her pant leg revealed a pentagram etched into her skin with a cobra head protruding out of it. I asked if I could take a picture, because I had never seen anything like that before. This was a very unusual case, since most victims of Satanic Ritual Abuse (SRA) dissociate and only start to recover memories years later. She was going to church in the daytime and to satanic rituals at night.

Dabblers and Demons

A local television station had a Sunday afternoon program that dealt with a variety of issues. They asked if I would be a guest on their show. A policeman and counselor would be joining me, but the special guest was a lady flown in from another state who claimed that she was raised in a Satanist's home. She fled for her life when she was about 19 years old, and never contacted her parents or relatives again. Now in her late 50s, she was there to tell her story.

I was relieved to find out that the counselor was a Christian who had some experience working with those who had been ritually abused. The policeman was assigned to work on occult crimes. He was the Los Angeles "expert" on Satanism, but he was on a different page than the counselor and me. He dealt with dabblers who deface gravestones, and drug dealers who claim to be Satanists. These are dangerous and deceived people for sure, but not hard-core underground Satanists, which is a strict and secret society. The policeman started out a little cocky but was wise enough to realize that his knowledge was superficial. The lady was not a Christian but was relieved that the counselor and I not only believed her story but were able to validate her experiences, which isn't always the case.

After the show, I asked her what she was doing to protect herself. She sprinkled salt around her house and did other rituals. I told her that if she would become a Christian, she would have all the protection she needs in

Christ and have the support of the Christian community. Unfortunately, her escorts whisked her away before she could respond, and I never saw her again.

Friday the Thirteenth and Full Moons

On another occasion, I was counseling two ritual abuse victims when Friday the thirteenth coincided with a full moon. I had no prior knowledge of the spiritual significance of such occurrences, but both inquirers called me that week and complained of more than the usual spiritual harassment. A month later two policemen stopped by my office. Their pastor was a former student of mine, and he encouraged them to meet with me. During the week prior to that Friday the thirteenth, a nineteen-year-old woman walked into their police station and said that she feared for her life. She claimed that her parents were Satanists, and she believed that she was going to be sacrificed that Friday evening. Fortunately, the woman behind the desk was a Christian and a friend of these two officers whom she called for assistance.

They didn't know whether to believe her or not but chose to err on the side of safety. The female officer went undercover with the young lady to the Friday evening ritual, with the two other officers standing by. Pandemonium broke out and she called for backup. They actually caught the girl's father and uncle in chargeable occult crimes and arrested them. The female officer took a leave of absence just to be with the young lady who still feared for her life. The two policemen asked me what I thought about their experience.

I cautioned them on two points. First, people like that are going to divulge a lot of information about the dark side and identify influential people. Harry, who I had spoken of earlier, shared the names of high-level people in politics and business, but it is almost better that you don't hear that. There is no way you can prove whether that is true or not, and you certainly can't act upon it unless you have actual evidence. However, you should believe them for the sake of helping them repent but learn from the experience and keep the information confidential.

Second, I told the policemen that it is highly unlikely that such cases will ever get to trial. They were surprised and said, "You're right. The uncle committed suicide in his cell and her father pleaded guilty on the grounds of insanity." That was the only case I know of where Satanists were actually caught in the middle of their ritual sacrifices.

Dissociative Identity Disorder

I had no prior instruction or experience with Dissociative Identity Disorder (DID)[28], so I was ill-prepared for my first exposure to it. That happened when a middle-aged lady in my office suddenly looked at me, said, "Who are you? Where am I? I'm getting out of here," and left. That freaked me out. I had been startled by demonic interruptions, but never frightened by them. This was different, and I asked myself, "What was that?" The next day the lady called and said, "I think I was in your office yesterday. What happened after that?" I wondered the same thing!

I had never seen someone switch personalities right in front of me before. It is an incredible experience. Everything about them changes. It appears that two or more totally different people share the same body. The personalities may or may not be co-conscious with each other. Every SRA victim that I have dealt with had DID, except for one, and she was the most pitiful person I have ever met. A secular diagnosis would likely be a schizoaffective disorder, because she was plagued by voices, and had zero ability to show any emotion. She couldn't cry, laugh, or smile.

An older lady was talking to me about her two children who were diagnosed with DID and she had no idea how that could have happened. She also had a question about herself. She couldn't cry, even though her tear ducts seemed to be okay. I said, "This may not make any sense to you, but just say aloud, "I renounce the lie that my crying would cause injury or death to myself or anyone else." As soon as she said that tears began to well up in her eyes. She too had been ritually abused. Such conditioning takes place during their rituals.

Satanic ritual abuse victims have been subjected to such extreme cruelty that they dissociate to survive. That allows the person to have a relatively normal development, but like any other defense mechanism it breaks down as they mature. Most will start to recall memories later on in life, which reflects the graciousness of God. He waits until they have enough maturity and support before He reveals their past experiences. Even then it will be traumatic, but they are in a better position to deal with the abuse. I call it the onion effect. Rather than reveal all their past at one time, God peels off one layer at a time. God will probably not reveal further hidden things if we don't take responsibility for what we already know.

Satanic Worship

Victims' stories started to make more sense to me when I realized that satanic worship is the antithesis of Christian worship. Our name is written in the Lamb's book of life, so they will write their name in blood in the goat's book of life. We are the bride of Christ and so they are wed to Satan. Victims need to renounce all ceremonies and assignments and announce their commitment to Christ. *The Steps* have satanic renunciations in the appendix. Most believers will experience no interference saying them aloud, but those who have been exposed to Satanism will have immediate opposition. Such victims can start their recovery by renouncing satanic lies and assignments and announcing true Christian worship as follows:

I renounce ever signing my name over to Satan or having my name signed over to Satan.

I announce that my name is now written in the Lamb's book of life (Revelation 3:5; 20:15).

I renounce any ceremony in which I have been wed to Satan.

I announce that I am the bride of Christ (Ephesians 5:32; Revelation 19:7).

I renounce any and all covenants I made with Satan.

I announce that I am alive in Christ and under the new covenant of grace (2 Corinthians 3:6).

I renounce all satanic assignments for my life, including duties, marriage, and children.

I announce and commit myself to know and do only the will of God (Matthew 7:21–23).

I renounce all spirit guides assigned to me.

I accept only the leading of the Holy Spirit (1 John 4:1–6).

I renounce ever giving my blood in the service of Satan.

I trust only the blood of the Lord Jesus Christ to save me (Revelation 1:5).

I renounce ever eating flesh or drinking blood for satanic worship.

I acknowledge only the flesh and blood of the Lord Jesus Christ in Holy Communion (1 Corinthians 10:14–21).

I renounce all guardians and Satanist parents who were assigned to me.

I announce that God is my Father, and the Holy Spirit is my guardian by whom I am sealed.

I renounce any baptism whereby I have been identified with Satan.

I announce that I have been baptized into Christ Jesus (1 Corinthians 12:13).

I renounce any and all sacrifices that were made on my behalf by which Satan may claim ownership of me.

I announce that only the sacrifice of Christ has any hold on me. I belong to Jesus.

Satanists are people who work in league with the demonic hierarchy of this world, just as Christians are people who work in league with the Holy Spirit who guides and empowers them. We are the wheat, and they are the tares, sown there by the devil (Matthew 13:37-42). Wheat and tares (*darnel*) look alike when they are young, but only the wheat will bear fruit. Tares propagate underground.

Terror at Night

I am thankful that God exposed me to this dark side of life before I conducted my first conference on "Resolving Personal and Spiritual Conflicts." The music director in the church started each session with a song and then left with his wife, which I couldn't help but notice. It turned out that they were going to his office and listening to my presentation. The next week they asked to see me and shared their story. Her parents had given her up to be raised by a wealthy man who became her ward. She went to a Catholic parochial school and was expected to get perfect grades, which she did. She would steal chalices and crucifixes from the church that her ward would use in satanic rituals in the basement of his mansion. She said he had a hotline phone to Washington and socialized with the highest levels of society. Three times she was "bred" to a young man and became pregnant. The fetuses were sacrificed. It is because of their innocence that fetuses and baby animals are sacrificed in an attempt to imitate our sinless Savior. The greater the innocence, the greater the power.

Near the end of her senior year of high school, she came back to the mansion after school as she normally would, but this time federal agents surrounded it. She was questioned for a month and finally released. She never saw her ward again. She eventually graduated from college with perfect grades, but her real talent was singing, which she pursued. She was nearly forty when she strolled into a small boutique and a Christian saleswoman invited her to church. That was the beginning of a long and painful recovery. After receiving Christ, she started having flashbacks of those early years.

She always wondered what happened to that boy that she was bred with, and to her shock, he showed up one day in the same church interviewing for the position of music director. Initially, she thought he was an infiltrator, so she kept out of his sight. Then one day she stepped out of the shadows and said to him, "Do you remember me?" He didn't at first, but that was enough to trigger his memories. He too had been subjected to Satanism, but his recovery was even more painful. At first, he hated her for being the one who opened up about his past, but that changed over time, and they eventually married.

After hearing their story, I said, "Good grief, what were you thinking when I came to your church?" They said, "You're the only one we felt safe enough to share our story with." At the time I was frequently being awakened at 3:00 AM, as were others that I was working with. I asked them, "What is the deal with 3:00 AM?" They told me that satanic rituals begin at midnight and continue to 3:00 AM, which is like prime time for demonic activity. I was just being targeted, and I was thankful that I already knew that "greater is He who is within me than he who is in the world." If you did nothing about it, the harassment would end at 4:00 AM. They showed me their wedding bands that had four diamonds on them to show the completion of demonic activity, and one for each child. The first three were sacrificed and now they have their own.

I have asked two questions during my conferences over the years. First, "How many of you have been suddenly awakened at a precise time in the morning, like 3:00 AM?" At least a third of the people would raise their hands. Second, "How many have awakened to an overwhelming sense of fear? It could have felt like you were half-asleep. You may have felt pressure on your chest or felt like something was grabbing your throat. You tried to do or say something but couldn't." Again, at least a third of the people would raise their hands. That is a direct spiritual attack, similar to what is described in Job 4:12-17:

> Now a word was brought to me stealthily; my ear received the whisper of it. Amid thoughts from visions of the night, when deep sleep falls on men, dread came upon me, and trembling, which made all my bones shake. A spirit glided past my face; the hair of my flesh stood up. It stood still, but I could discern its appearance. A form was before my eyes; there was silence, then I heard a voice; "Can mortal man be in the right before God? Can a man be pure before his Maker?

The phrase, "a word was brought to me," is not a word from the Lord. This was a message from the accuser of the brethren. I experienced the same attack every night before I started a conference, and it continued from 1990 to 1994. I struggled at first until I learned how to deal with it. The natural response is to try to say something or to do something physical, but "the weapons of our warfare are not of the flesh but have divine power to destroy strongholds" (2 Corinthians 10:4). I was trying to overcome the attack physically, which will not work against the powers of darkness. "For everyone who calls upon the name of the Lord will be saved" (Romans 10:13), but I couldn't verbally call upon the Lord, and I knew that Satan is under no obligation to obey my thoughts, since he doesn't perfectly know them. The order of Scripture is critical. We must first "submit to God and then resist the devil" (James 4:7). We don't have to say anything with our mouth to submit to God, since He knows "the thoughts and intentions of our hearts" (Hebrews 4:12). Turning to God inwardly freed me to say out loud, "Jesus," and the attack would stop. I believe God allows that for our testing. We can struggle on our own, or we can submit to God.

Preach the Gospel

I was not looking for these experiences, but God was bringing them to me for a purpose. He showed me the dark side of reality. and I came to a very important conclusion. The kingdom of darkness is part of this fallen world, but it is not the task of the Church to defeat Satan. Jesus has already disarmed him. We are called to teach and preach the gospel. I also had to decide whether I was called to be a caregiver to the ritua ly abused, which takes a huge amount of time, or focus on equipping the church. I chose the latter.

My experiences were not isolated or uncommon, which I became aware of as I traveled around the country. Of the Christian leaders who attended the advanced portion of my conference, a third of them were trying to help ritual abuse victims. The most important lessons I learned had to do with the battle for our minds. We can't read each other's minds, so we have no idea what people are struggling with unless they tell us. Most people are not likely to do that. Consequently, many struggle alone, thinking they are the only ones who have such problems. They will readily share what others have done to them but remain silent about their mental battles. Some churches will deny these struggles and provide no instruction to help them. The fact that it is so easily resolved is the real tragedy. The primary evangelistic appeal of the early church was to offer freedom from spiritual bondage, and being able to help them was a test of orthodoxy.

Demons are like cockroaches, they only come out in the darkness. When the lights come on, they scurry for the shadows. Their first strategy is to avoid detection. If their cover is exposed, they will resort to some pretense of power to intimidate those who are trying to help. If encouragers respond in fear, they are operating in the flesh and the demons are safe. Nothing gets resolved. The key is to bring those thoughts out of darkness and into the light. The whole battle is deception, which is why truth sets us free.

Satan's Schemes

On one occasion I could tell that an inquirer was being distracted, and I asked, "What are you hearing now?" She said, "They are laughing at you." My poor feeble efforts were accomplishing nothing but to make me an object of ridicule! The first time I heard that I was a little intimidated until I realized the strategy. It was like little children behind a fence taunting those who walk by because they think they are safe. If the person finds a gap in the fence, the kids run for their lives. When I exposed that strategy, the laughter stopped.

Some inquirers have told me that they never even considered the option of not obeying or believing those thoughts. Others have trouble separating their thoughts from the enemy's thoughts. Leading them through *The Steps* will help them clarify that. One lady insisted on her husband being present, which I usually don't recommend because in all likelihood he would be one of many she would need to forgive. But she needed his presence for emotional support. She had been severely abused and had trouble maintaining control at first. During the process, she looked up and said with a smile on her face, "Do you know what I am hearing now?" It didn't matter what she was hearing, the battle was over. She clearly understood that those were not her thoughts, and she didn't have to pay attention to them anymore. Her mind was quiet when the appointment was over.

Some of these mental thoughts are very subtle. I was doing a conference in Austria. A Godly theologian shared his struggle afterward. Every time he looked at men, he inadvertently looked at their crotch. It had been going on since he was in his early twenties. At first, I thought he was struggling with homosexuality, but when I probed in that direction, he clearly said that was not his problem. He told a doctor about it and got a prescription, but he knew that wasn't the answer. For years he had been wondering, "What in the world is wrong with me?" I asked him, "What do you believe now after hearing my presentation?" He said, "There is nothing wrong with me. I'm a heterosexual male child of God." I said, "Exactly, and what should you do about it from now on?" He said, "Just don't pay attention to it, and it will eventually subside."

A Godly psychologist friend shared a similar experience. For three out of his five years of doctoral studies, he struggled with a bizarre thought. Every time he had a cup of coffee in his hand and was talking to another person, he would have this impulsive thought to throw it in their face. He never did, but for three years he wondered what was wrong with him.

When I first started doing public conferences, I had an unusual experience that went on for four years. I would conclude the conference by leading them through *The Steps*. When I went to the podium a very clear thought would come to my mind. "There is a gun pointed at your head." Now if that thought was from God, I should have ducked. But it would not instill any confidence in the congregation if I were ducking around trying to avoid invisible bullets. I must admit that I did casually look around the first time that happened, but never again.

Suppose a mother comes home from the hospital with her third child. She is alone at home and the newborn is crying and the other children are acting up. She is exhausted and suddenly she has a thought, "Kill your babies." Who is she going to share that thought with? Imagine her husband coming home that evening, and she says, "Hi honey, I have had thoughts about killing the kids!" That is not going to happen. Almost every time I used that illustration in a conference, some mother has come up afterward and said, "That has been happening to me." Do they kill their babies? The vast majority don't, of course, but some do. A mother in Texas drowned five of her babies, and she knew it was demonic, but the courts didn't. She was found guilty and pleaded insanity due to post-partum depression. The vast majority who don't kill their babies are left feeling guilty for having such thoughts. The church is failing these people who desperately need to know the truth that will set them free.

I was speaking at a camp when the director woke me up at 1:00 a.m. saying, "We need you in the kitchen." Someone had broken into the pantry from the outside. As we walked toward the kitchen, I could see two men at one end of a table, but I didn't see the third person until I stepped through the door. He was the assistant cook, and he was holding a butcher's knife to his throat. The first words out of his mouth were, "This so-and-so is going to die tonight." What would you do?

I sat down beside him and said, "No he's not." I said to him, "I know you can hear me now. This is just a voice in your head. You can believe it if you want and continue holding that knife to your throat, or you can choose not to believe it, and put the knife down." He struggled a little and said, "Is that all it is?" I said, "Well, isn't it? There is no physical force in this room controlling you. You are just paying attention to a deceiving spirit." He put the knife down and asked, "If I go to bed will you help me tomorrow?" I told him I would, and he reached under his seat and pulled out an even bigger knife and put it on the table. We gave each other a hug, and off he went to bed.

Man of Lawlessness

The wheat and the tares co-exist on planet earth, and in the end, the antichrist will rule over the world.

> "It was given to him to make war with the saints and to overcome them, and authority over every tribe and people and tongue and nation was given to him. All who dwell on the earth will worship him, everyone whose name has not been written from the foundation of the world in the book of life of the Lamb who has been slain" (Revelation 13:7,8).

This is no time to compromise who we are. We must stand firm in our faith, win as many as we can to Christ, and help liberate and heal the wounds of those who have been held captive by Satan to do his will.

I was conducting a conference when the forty-year-old daughter of the previous pastor asked for help. She couldn't process anything on her own, and she had been in counseling for twenty years. I told her to get what she could out of the conference, and I would see her the following Monday. She had been raped by a counselor twenty years previously and had no memory of life before that. I asked her to read through the "Satanic Renunciations," which she couldn't do. I was able to help her forgive that counselor, and that started a whole parade of memories of ritual abuse. One of her personalities was like a little child. When that personality came forward, she got off her chair, sat on the floor, and said, "It is too bright in here." I watched as her pupils dilated. She said, "Who are you?" I said, "I'm your friend." Whenever she showed up, she would say, "Hi mister friend."

Another personality was extremely hostile and said, "Don't you know that I could make a phone call, and, in an hour, you would be dead?" I said, "There is the phone. Make the call." I asked that personality, "Why do you serve a god that wants you to sacrifice for him? I serve a God who sacrificed for me." I never saw that personality again. Thankfully, this courageous lady was fully integrated and gave me a Christmas present. It was a wreath made from grape vines and in the middle was the following poem:

The Wreath

A friend of mine whose grapevine died had put it out for
trash.

I said to her, "I'll take that vine and make something of that."

At home, the bag of dead, dry vines looked nothing but a
mess.

But as I gently bent one vine entwining 'round and 'round,

A rustic wreath began to form, potential did abound.

One vine would not go where it should, and anxious as I
was,

I forced it so to change its shape, it broke – and what the
cause?

If I had taken precious time to slowly change its form,

It would have made a lovely wreath, not a dead vine, broken,
torn.

As I finished bending, adding blooms, applying trim,

I realized how that rustic wreath is like my life within.

You see, so many in my life have tried to make me change.

They've forced my spirit anxiously, I tried to rearrange.

I plunged far deeper in despair, my spirit broken, torn.

Then God allowed a gentle one that knew of dying vines,

To kindly, patiently allow the Lord to take His time.

And though the vine has not yet formed a decorative wreath,

I know that with God's servant's help one day when Christ I
meet,

He'll see a finished circle, a wreath with all the trim.

So, as you look upon this gift, the vine round and complete,

Remember God is using you to gently shape His wreath.

Discussion Questions

1. Why should we never make deals with the devil?
2. What is the difference between someone who is spiritually deceived and a Satanist?
3. What are DID and SRA?
4. In what ways is Satanic worship the antithesis of Christian worship?
5. How can you overcome night terrors?
6. What should the main thrust of the Church be?
7. Why does Satan try to frighten believers?
8. What are Satan's schemes?
9. Why don't most believers share what they are mentally struggling with?
10. How can or can't the wheat and the tares co-exist?

Chapter Seven: Spiritual Discernment

"We must carefully discern the thoughts that come on us and set them against the testimonies from the divinely inspired Scriptures and from the teaching of the spiritual teachers, the holy Fathers, so that, if we find them to agree with these witnesses and correspond to them, we may with all our might hold fast these thoughts and boldly act on them. But if they are not in harmony with "the word of truth" we must expel them from us with much anger, as it is written, "Be angry, but sin not." As from something defiling and from the sting of death, so must we flee from the interior assault of passionate thoughts. Accordingly, we need great soberness, great zeal and much searching of the divine Scriptures. The Savior has shown us their usefulness by saying, "search the Scriptures." Search them and hold fast to what they say with great exactitude and faith, in order that you may know God's will clearly from the divine Scriptures and be able infallibly to distinguish good from evil and not believe every spirit."[29]

Symeon the New Theologian

A good friend of mine and his wife were missionaries. Their missionary group had invited an authoritarian pastor to speak at several of their events. After hearing him speak so persuasively, my friends decided to attend his church and to see him for counseling. The wife had reservations, but they continued seeing him anyway. Over the next year their ministry and marriage deteriorated, as well as our friendship. Later, this wolf in sheep's clothing was exposed for having sex with a number of students in their mission. He justified his behavior by explaining, "What we do in the flesh doesn't matter. Only what we do in the spirit counts." That is a contemporary form of Gnosticism, a dualistic teaching that matter is inherently evil and can have no contact with God. In Gnosticism Jesus only appeared to be a man and suffered in appearance only. This "enlightened knowledge" was supposed to help discern good from evil, but the apostle John explained that it did just the opposite.

"For many deceivers have gone out into the world, those who do not acknowledge Jesus Christ as coming in the flesh. This is the deceiver and the antichrist" (2 John 7).

"Little children, let no one deceive you; the one who practices righteousness is righteous, just as he is righteous: the one who practices sin is of the devil" (1 John 3:7,8).

My friend was given an ultimatum: choose to stay with the mission or choose the "pastor." He chose to stay with the deceiver, and it ended his marriage and ministry. He didn't initially exercise spiritual discernment nor judge righteously in the end. I tried to persuade him, but con men have a mesmerizing hold over their followers. Spiritual discernment is our first line of defense. When we have a check in our spirit, as the wife did, we must not ignore it. We are living in deceptive times, and the need to be discerning can't be overstated.

Self-deception is the most difficult to deal with, because the individual doesn't realize they have deceived themselves. That is the point that James is making;

> "But prove yourselves doers of the word, and not merely hearers who delude themselves. For if anyone is a hearer of the word and not a doer, he is like a man who looks at his natural face in a mirror; for once he has looked at himself and gone away, he has immediately forgotten what kind of person he was" (James 1:22-24).

If you live a lie long enough, after a while you believe it to be true.

Ethics and Morality

Everyone has a conscience that has been shaped by the environment in which they are raised. It is a function of their minds. A conscience is always true to itself, but not necessarily to the Word of God. Letting your conscience be your guide is an ethical standard for the world, but not for the believer. Even non-believers think it is hypocritical to violate one's own conscience. Ethics is the science of determining right from wrong, whereas morality is measured by the ability to live up to those standards. Ethical standards for unbelievers are different than for believers, which is why they can promote homosexuality and abortion without violating their conscience.

A politician was confronted for lying about a candidate that he supported. He shrugged it off by saying, "She won!" For him, the end justified the means, which is situational ethics. He showed no remorse about lying, because it didn't violate his conscience. But it should violate the conscience of a believer. "Let us do evil that good may come. Their condemnation is just" (Romans 3:8). So don't be surprised when unbelievers live by a different moral code. Unbelievers are likely "paying attention to deceitful spirits and doctrines of demons, by means of the hypocrisy of liars seared in their own conscience as with a branding iron" (1 Timothy 4:1,2). Unbelievers are in league with the father of lies, which is why they are unlikely to apologize. It's not wrong according to their standards.

Spiritually Renewed Minds

Believers have a conscience that needs to be renewed to God's standards. It will take time to be transformed by the renewing of their minds, but from the beginning of their Christian journey, believers have the Holy Spirit to guide them and convict them of wrongdoing. One will have to question their salvation if they sense no conviction when they sin. The major function of the Holy Spirit is to communicate God's presence to His children as shared in 1 Corinthians 2:9-16:

> But just as it is written: "Things which eye has not seen and ear has not heard, And which have not entered the human heart, All that God has prepared for those who love Him." For to us God revealed them through the Spirit; for the Spirit searches all things, even the depths of God. For who among people knows the thoughts of a person except the spirit of the person that is in him? So also the thoughts of God no one knows, except the Spirit of God. Now we have not received the spirit of the world, but the Spirit who is from God, so that we may know the things freely given to us by God. We also speak these things, not in words taught by human wisdom, but in those taught by the Spirit, combining spiritual thoughts with spiritual words. But a natural person does not accept the things of the Spirit of God, for they are foolishness to him; and he cannot understand them, because they are spiritually discerned. But the one who is spiritual discerns all things, yet he himself is discerned by no one. For who has known the mind of the Lord, that he will instruct Him? But we have the mind of Christ.

What should we learn from this passage? First, a natural man cannot discern what is spiritually true; he can only know his own thoughts and that which he can perceive through his natural senses.

Second, the Holy Spirit knows all things and is capable of revealing the nature of God and His will. The Spirit of God knows the thoughts of God, because they are one and the same.

Third, we have not received the spirit of the world but the Spirit that is from God. The Holy Spirit makes known to us the things freely given by God.

Fourth, we have the mind of Christ, because He indwells us. Our bodies are His temple.

Fifth, the Holy Spirit takes words (logos), which are not taught by human wisdom but by the Spirit, and combines (brings together, compares, or explains) them. What is actually being combined or compared isn't clear. The original language literally reads, "spirituals with spirituals." The NASB translates the phrase: "...combining spiritual thoughts with spiritual words." The NIV translates the phrase: "...words taught by the Spirit, expressing the spiritual truths in spiritual words."

John Chrysostom wrote of this passage in the fourth century:

> If the Spirit, who knows the secret things of God, had not revealed them to us, there is no way that we could ever have known them... God gave us a mind in order that we might learn and receive help from Him, not in order that the mind should be self-sufficient. If my soul chooses to see without the Spirit, it becomes a danger to itself... We know the things which are in the mind of Christ, which He has willed and revealed to us. That does not mean that we know everything which Christ knows but rather that everything which we know comes from Him and is spiritual.[30]

"In reference to your former manner of life, you lay aside the old self, which is being corrupted in accordance with the lusts of deceit, and that you be renewed in the spirit of your mind and put on the new self, which in the likeness of God has been created in righteousness and holiness of the truth" (Ephesians 4:22-24). God communicates to us through the means of our own faculties. When someone says, "God really spoke to me last night," they are not saying they heard an audible voice. They believe their thinking was inspired by God. The voice of God resonates with our spirit resulting in a peaceful conclusion.

The problem is, we can't think beyond our own vocabulary. There is a limit to what a father can communicate to a five-year-old. The more we understand Scripture and the meaning of God's Word, the more He can combine spiritual thoughts with spiritual words. Therefore, we should let the word of Christ richly dwell within us so He can rule in our hearts (see Colossians 3:15,16). Those who have done so are in a position to discern good and evil.

Discerning Right from Wrong

In the Old Testament, the Hebrew word bin is used 247 times and is translated as "discern," "distinguish" and occasionally "understand." It means "to make a distinction or separate from." The New Testament counterpart, *diakrino*, also means "to separate or divide." It is used primarily in reference to making righteous decisions. The Holy Spirit enables us to distinguish right from wrong, truth from lies, and God's thoughts from human thoughts.

When David died, Solomon took his place as king of Israel, but he was young and inexperienced. He prayed, "And now, O Lord my God, Thou has made Thy servant king in place of my father David, yet I am but a little child;

I do not know how to go out or come in" (1 Kings 3:7). The Lord appeared to Solomon in a dream at night and said, "Ask what you wish Me to give you." Solomon gave his request and the Lord responded as follows:

> And Your servant is in the midst of Your people whom You have chosen, a great people who are too many to be numbered or counted. So, give Your servant an understanding heart to judge Your people, to discern between good and evil. For who is capable of judging this great people of Yours?" Now it was pleasing in the sight of the Lord that Solomon had asked this thing. And God said to him, "Because you have asked this thing, and have not asked for yourself a long life, nor have asked riches for yourself, nor have you asked for the lives of your enemies, but have asked for yourself discernment to understand justice, behold, I have done according to your words. Behold, I have given you a wise and discerning heart, so that there has been no one like you before you, nor shall one like you arise after you (1 Kings 3:8-12).

This passage reveals several key concepts about discernment. First, God gave Solomon the ability to discern because of the purity of his motives. Solomon wasn't asking for personal gain or an advantage over his enemies. He was asking for the ability to discern between good and evil, and God gave it to him. The Lord does not enable us to exercise the mind of Christ with wrong motives coming from an impure heart. The same holds for the exercise of any spiritual gift. Wrong motives open the door for Satan's counterfeits.

When I was teaching at Talbot School of Theology, I couldn't help but notice that an undergraduate student was following me around to various speaking engagements. After an evening service, she was visibly shaken. I encouraged her to stop by my office the next day. From the beginning of her enrollment, she had been seeing a counselor on campus. I asked her how that was going. She said it was like a game and she told me everything the counselor was going to do in their next session. I said, "You like doing that, don't you? You like the advantage it gives you over other people." As soon as I exposed the deception, an evil spirit surfaced.

She believed God had given her a spiritual gift that enabled her to identify people's sins. She could point out students that were struggling with sexual sins, and various other problems. As far as I could tell, she was right. Yet when she found her freedom in Christ, the ability disappeared. That wasn't the Holy Spirit enabling her to discern. It was an evil spirit compatible with the evil spirits that were related to the moral problems in other people. Throughout church history that has been referred to as a "familiar spirit." Her goal was to be a Christian counselor and use this "gift" to "help" others. Thankfully she found her freedom in Christ and became a missionary in Africa.

Second, the passage from 1 Kings reveals that true biblical discernment is on the plane of good and evil. The "distinguishing of spirits" mentioned in 1 Corinthians 12:10 is the God-given ability to distinguish between the Holy Spirit and evil spirits. Two missionaries asked me to help a young student who was plagued by compulsive thoughts that contributed to an eating disorder. As she was going through the process of forgiving others, I discerned that it wasn't the girl speaking anymore. "That's not her," I said. The expression on her face changed, and a different voice said, "She will never forgive that person." In this case, my discernment was right. After the session, they asked how I knew it was the wrong spirit. There is no natural way to explain it, but I knew in my spirit, because of God's presence in my life. She did forgive that person. After finding her freedom in Christ, she too is now working as a missionary.

Practicing Discernment

Spiritual discernment is divine enablement and complements what we can know and distinguish with our minds. We evaluate what we see and hear with our minds, but that has limits. For instance, a Satanist has no problem lying and could give you a statement of faith that your mind agrees with, and you would be deceived without the ability to discern. The mind cannot always tell when someone is lying, but a check in your spirit indicates that something is wrong. The mind wants to know what's wrong, but we may not always know that. The Holy Spirit enables us to discern that something is wrong, but not necessarily what is wrong.

Suppose a boy comes home and the father senses he did something wrong. So, he asks, "What's wrong, son?" The boy says, "Nothing!" He asks again what's wrong, and again the boy claims nothing is wrong. The father was correct in discerning that something wasn't right, but he could misuse what he discerned by suggesting what the problem is. "Son, have you been doing such and such again?" If the guess is wrong, he will blow the discernment. The boy will walk away feeling angry that he was falsely accused.

So, what should we do when we don't know what is wrong? Just share the discernment. "Son, something is wrong." "No, Dad, nothing's wrong!" "Son, I know something is wrong." The boy shrugs his shoulders and goes to his room. Is that the end of it? Only if there is no God! The Holy Spirit enabled the discernment and will convict the boy if he sinned. Now the boy is probably thinking, *"Dad knows!"* The dad doesn't know what the boy did, and therefore can't discipline him, because discipline has to be based on observed behavior. But the boy's Heavenly Father will discipline him out of love in order that he may share in His holiness.

I was beginning a conference on a Sunday morning and between the two services I said to the pastor, "Do you want to talk about what is going on in the church?" He said, "Is it that obvious?" It was to me. The air was so thick you could cut it with a knife. The pastoral staff was deeply divided, two against the other two. <u>The whole atmosphere changed Monday evening after I talked about forgiveness.</u> It was so noticeable that people throughout the week were commenting on the change.

Growing in Discernment

Have you ever been in a public setting and noticed a total stranger giving you an icy stare? I have numerous times. In one case I started walking toward the person and he immediately got up and left. We didn't share a compatible spirit. On the other hand, have you sensed a compatible spirit with a stranger and "knew" they were a believer without a word being spoken? The ability to discern increases with our maturity according to Hebrews 5:12 - 6:2:

> For though by this time, you ought to be teachers, you have need again for someone to teach you the elementary principles of the actual words of God, and you have come to need milk and not solid food. For everyone who partakes only of milk is unacquainted with the word of righteousness, for he is an infant. But solid food is for the mature, who because of practice have their senses trained to distinguish between good and evil. Therefore leaving the elementary teaching about the Christ, let us press on to maturity, not laying again a foundation of repentance from dead works and of faith toward God, of instruction about washings and laying on of hands, and about the resurrection of the dead and eternal judgment.

What the writer of Hebrews identifies as elementary teaching is advanced theology for some people. A good systematic theology is the foundation upon which we build our lives. It is to our walk with God what our skeleton is to our body. It holds us together and keeps us in the right form, but it is the Holy Spirit who gives life to the body (Romans 8:11). Those accustomed to the word of righteousness are sensitive to the personal leading of the Holy Spirit enabling them to discern good from evil.

Discernment is not A Replacement for Scriptural Knowledge

The Holy Spirit does more than warn us. He enables us to understand Scripture and enhances our spiritual understanding so that we can effectively minister to others. As I have matured in the Lord, I find that these impressions get to the heart of the issue when ministering to others. However, such impressions are not a substitute for knowing the Bible, and they need to be tested as I mentioned in an earlier chapter. Our ability to discern grows in proportion to our spiritual maturity and knowledge of God and His ways. God brings to our minds the Scripture we have already put into our hearts. There are no shortcuts to maturity. The Holy Spirit enables us to discern, but it comes in the context of showing compassion, developing trusting relationships, and exercising patience. The leading of the Holy Spirit works through the whole counsel of God.

Deceiving spirits encourage shortcuts, bypass the mind, and seek to create a dependency upon esoteric knowledge (knowledge that does not come through our normal channels of perception or disciplined study). You won't even have to think. Just go by whatever thought pops into your mind. That's how mediums and psychics work. WRONG

God will also bring to your mind what you have learned from His Word. Countless times I have recalled passages that I haven't thought about in years when ministering to people. Jesus said:

> "Do not worry beforehand about what you are to say but say whatever is given you in that hour; for it is not you who speak, but it is the Holy Spirit" (Mark 13:11).

Binding and Loosing

Jesus said to Peter, "I will give you the keys of the kingdom of heaven: and whatever you bind on earth shall have been bound in heaven, and whatever you loose on earth shall have been loosed in heaven" (Matthew 16:19). Jesus said to the Pharisees, "You have taken away the key of knowledge; you yourselves did not enter and hindered those who were entering" (Luke 11:52). The keys to the kingdom of heaven are the knowledge of what we can legally bind and loose. A.T. Robertson wrote, "To 'bind' in rabbinical language is to forbid; to 'loose' is to permit."[31] Binding was a declaration that anything unlawful could not be done. Loosing was a declaration that anything lawful could be done. The Pharisees were forbidding themselves and others from entering the kingdom of God by declaring Jesus as unlawful.

One difficulty in understanding Matthew 16:19 and 18:18 is the translation. The NASB reads, "Whatever you bind on earth shall have been bound in heaven, and whatever you loose on earth shall have been loosed in heaven." The NIV reads, "Whatever you bind on earth will be bound in heaven, and whatever you loose on earth will be loosed in heaven." The Greek text can be translated either way. The same linguistic problem occurs in the gospel of John when Jesus breathed on His disciples and said, "Receive the Holy Spirit. If you forgive the sins of any, their sins have been forgiven them; if you retain the sin of any, they have been retained" (20:22,23 NASB). The NIV reads, "Receive the Holy Spirit. If you forgive anyone his sins, they are forgiven; if you do not forgive them, they are not forgiven." Obviously, God does not forgive people's sin because we do or don't. For centuries Christians have confessed their sins during worship and priests have assured them of God's pardoning grace often quoting 1 John 1:9. The priest isn't forgiving them. He is just declaring that God already has.

Binding (forbidding), loosing (permitting), and forgiving of sins are what God has authorized the Church to do and proclaim under His authority. Matthew offers the following safeguard to ensure that we don't overstep our authority: "Again I say to you, that if two of you agree on earth about anything that they may ask, it shall be done for them by my Father who is in heaven. For where two or three have gathered together in my name, I am there in their midst" (Matthew 18:19,20) The two or three are agreeing together on what they know to be true, what they are hearing from God, and then announcing it. Maybe that is why God established a plurality of elders to oversee spiritual ministries. What we agree together in the natural realm (on earth) affects the spiritual realm (in heaven). Recall from chapter one "that the manifold wisdom of God might now be made known through the church to the rulers and the authorities in the heavenly realm" (Ephesians 3:10).

Before church board and committee meetings, and all church services the spiritual leadership should agree together and profess verbally that Satan is bound, i.e., that he and his demons are not granted permission to inflict any harm, speak any lies, or blind the mind of the unbelieving. We have the authority to do God's will, so why not exercise it?

I was conducting a conference in India when a young missionary asked for personal help. He was under psychiatric care at the time, which was very embarrassing to him. He had gone into Hindu temples with the intent of casting out the demons, but he ended up being the victim. He asked me why that didn't work. I said, "You had no authority to do that. Those temples don't belong to you. Believers have to be submissive to the governing authority of the country they are in (see Romans 12:1), and you weren't." You can only be a good steward of what God has entrusted to you, but not for what He has entrusted to somebody else.

I have stayed in a lot of hotels over the years, and only God knows what has gone on in those rooms beforehand. If I want to have a good night's rest, I spiritually cleanse that room by verbally renouncing anything that has happened in that room in the past that did not please God. Then by the authority and power of the Lord Jesus Christ, I command every evil spirit to leave, and I ask Almighty God to put a hedge of protection around the room as long as I occupy it. I have the right to do that since I am submissive to the laws of the land and have legally contracted to rent that room. Before I start a conference or any speaking engagement, I pray the following with those who are responsible for the service:

> Lord, I declare my dependency upon You, for apart from You I can do nothing. I commit my body to You as a living sacrifice, and I ask You to fill me with Your Holy Spirit and superintend my choice of words. Together, we commit this

time and place to You and agree together that Satan and all evil spirits are bound in this auditorium. In Jesus' name I pray. Amen.

I have yet to see any interference during any of my conferences.

CRU, formerly Campus Crusade for Christ, has asked me several times to speak on college campuses about demonic activity in the world. I made sure that they had been granted permission to use the room or auditorium. Therefore, we had a legal right to be there, and we had the authority to forbid the enemy from interfering. We prayed together as mentioned above, and you could hear a pin drop throughout the presentation.

When we lead people through *The Steps,* we have the inquirer pray and then make the following declaration:

> In the name and authority of the Lord Jesus Christ, I command Satan and all evil spirits to release their hold on me in order that I can be free to know and choose to do the will of God. As a child of God who is seated with Christ in the heavenly places, I declare that every enemy of the Lord Jesus Christ in my presence be bound. God has not given me a spirit of fear; therefore, I reject any and all condemning, accusing, blasphemous, and deceiving spirits of fear. Satan and all his demons cannot inflict any pain or in any way prevent God's will from being done in my life today, because I belong to the Lord Jesus Christ.

Such a declaration prevents the enemy from interfering with the repentance process. Notice that the inquirer is not telling them to leave. They do that after they have repented. The Accuser will claim squatters' rights, because of the ground the person has yielded to him, just as he did with Simon Peter. Jesus said, "Simon, Simon, Satan has demanded permission to sift you like wheat; but I have prayed for you, that your faith may not fail; and you, when once you have turned again, strengthen the brothers" (Luke 22:31,32). The context reveals that Simon Peter, and the other disciples were arguing as to which one of them "...was regarded to be greatest" (vs. 24). Satan was kicked out of heaven because of his pride so why shouldn't Peter have to suffer the same? Because Peter didn't compare himself with God as Satan had, but with the other disciples. Even so, Peter forfeited control of his life and denied Jesus three times. But he was convicted, and then repented and strengthened his brothers.

While on a conference tour, my beloved wife would start complaining as we approached the city of our destination. After the third time, it finally dawned on me what was happening. I verbally forbade the enemy to interfere with our mission, and it never happened again. A skeptical pastor enrolled in my Doctor of Ministry class and finished the week unconvinced.

To complete the course, he and his wife attended a "Setting Your Marriage Free" conference. A month later he reported that he and his wife had been bickering every Sunday morning before they went to church, and they would arrive in a bad mood. He had never considered that to be a spiritual attack until he took my class. He was no longer skeptical after experiencing four peaceful Sundays in a row. We should all have our senses trained to discern good and evil and then exercise our God-given authority for all Christian endeavors. Don't give Satan permission to interfere with your mission.

Discussion Questions

1. What is the difference between ethics and morality?
2. Why is letting our conscience be our guide insufficient for believers?
3. Why don't unbelievers sense any remorse when they say and do things that believers know are wrong?
4. What part of 2 Corinthians 2:9-16 impacted you the most? Why?
5. Why is motive a factor in discerning right from wrong?
6. Why is it still important to discern that something is wrong without knowing what is wrong?
7. How can we have our senses trained to discern good from evil?
8. What do binding and loosing mean?
9. Why is it so important to know the scope and limits of our authority and power in the spiritual realm?
10. How can you put into practice what you have learned in this chapter?

Chapter Eight: Praying by the Spirit

> Insofar as our conduct is right, we are rightly prepared for the Holy Spirit to abide in us. Hence, we are more ready to obtain what we request. This, therefore, is what it means to pray in the Spirit at all times. We are directing our prayer to God with a clean conscience and sincere faith. One who prays with a polluted mind prays only in the flesh, not in the Spirit.[32]
>
> *Ambrose, Epistle to the Ephesians 6:20*

I was taught as a new believer that prayer was communing with God, but the discipline of prayer was the most frustrating part of my early Christian experience. I read about great saints who would spend two, three or four hours a day in prayer – sometimes even all night! I was struggling to spend five minutes. I would labor through my prayer list for two or three minutes, and glance at my watch wondering what I would say the next two minutes. Prayer was supposed to be a dialogue with God, but most of the time it seemed like I was talking to the wall. If prayer is so important, why is it so difficult?

My greatest struggle was trying to stay focused. I would make a list of what I wanted to pray for, but distracting thoughts competed fiercely for my mind. Daily activities demanded my attention, and pesky thoughts would remind me of my many weaknesses. I assumed Satan was trying to distract me from my devotional life. If you are wondering if others experience the same difficulties, they are, even spiritual giants like A.B. Simpson who wrote a little booklet entitled, *Power of Stillness*[33]:

> A score of years ago, a friend placed in my hand a little book which became one of the turning points of my life. It was entitled, *True Peace.* It was an old medieval message, and it had but one thought, and it was this – that God was waiting in the depths of my being to talk to me if I would only get still enough to hear His voice. I thought this would be a very easy matter, and so I began to get still. But I had no sooner commenced than a perfect pandemonium of voices reached my ears, a thousand clamoring notes from without and within, until I could hear nothing but their noise and din.

Some of them were my own voice; some of them were my own questions, some of them were my own cares, some of them were my very prayers. Others were the suggestions of the tempter and the voices of the world's turmoil. Never before did there seem so many things to be done, to be said, to be thought; and in every direction, I was pushed and pulled, and greeted with noisy acclamations and unspeakable unrest. It seemed necessary for me to listen to some of them, and to answer some of them; but God said, "Be still, and know that I am God."

Then came the conflict of thoughts for tomorrow, and its duties and cares, but God said, "Be still." And as I listened, and slowly learned to obey, and shut my ears to every sound, I found after a while that when the other voices ceased, or I ceased to hear them, there was a still, small voice in the depths of my being that began to speak with an inexpressible, tenderness, power, and comfort. As I listened it became to me the voice of prayer, and the voice of wisdom, and the voice of duty, and I did not need to think so hard, but that "still, small voice" of the Holy Spirit in my heart was God's prayer in my secret soul; was God's answer to all my questions; was God's life and strength for soul and body, and became the substance of all knowledge, and all prayer, and all blessing; for it was the living God Himself as my life and my all.

The Key to Liberating Prayer

I was still a seminary student when my prayer life radically changed in one night. I was teaching a series of lessons on prayer to a group of college students. My resource was an old book I found on prayer. I read the first half of the book and thought it was theologically sound. So, I advertised the titles of each chapter in the book to be the subjects of my lessons that summer. Not too creative, but typical of young pastors whose reservoir of wisdom is quite shallow – we teach the notes of dead saints until we own the message ourselves! The last chapter was entitled, "How to Pray in the Spirit." I read it for the first time the night before I was supposed to teach it Sunday morning. Not very good preparation, and no reflection on the author, but after reading the chapter I didn't have the foggiest idea how to pray in the Spirit. I was hours away from giving a message I had not incorporated into my own life. I felt spiritually bankrupt.

I had all but given up trying to prepare a message and given in to plan B, which was to show a movie I saved for such moments. Then came Jesus! It was approaching midnight when the Lord began to direct my thoughts. My journey through the Bible that night turned out to be one of the most impactful experiences of my life. I began to reason, "If I'm going to pray in the Spirit, then I must be filled with the Spirit." So, I turned to Ephesians 5:18-20 (key portions are underlined in the following verses):

> Do not get drunk with wine, for that is dissipation, but be filled with the Spirit, speaking to one another in psalms, and hymns and spiritual songs, singing and making melody in your heart to the Lord; <u>always giving thanks</u> for all things in the name of our Lord Jesus Christ, even the Father.

Then I turned to the parallel passage in Colossians 3:15-17:

> Let the peace of Christ rule in your hearts, to which indeed you were called in one body; and <u>be thankful</u>. Let the word of Christ richly dwell within you, with all wisdom teaching and admonishing one another with psalms and hymns and spiritual songs, singing <u>with thankfulness</u> in your hearts to God. Whatever you do in word or deed, do all in the name of the Lord Jesus, <u>giving thanks</u> through Him to God the Father.

As a seminary student, I observed that being "filled with the Spirit" and "letting the word of Christ richly dwell" within us had the same results. But I had not previously observed that both were accompanied by an attitude of gratitude. I turned the page in my Bible to Colossians 4:2: "Devote yourselves to prayer, keeping alert in it with <u>an attitude of thanksgiving</u>." Then I recalled Philippians 4:6: "Be anxious for nothing, but in everything by prayer and supplication <u>with thanksgiving</u>..." This discovery opened my eyes as I turned to 1 Thessalonians 5:17-18: "Pray without ceasing; <u>in everything give thanks</u>; for this is God's will for you in Christ Jesus." Prayer and thanksgiving seemed to be inseparable. Like a little child finding another package under the Christmas tree – and another, and another. I discovered Paul's personal practices in his epistles as follows:

> I...do not cease giving thanks for you, while making mention of you in my prayers (Ephesians 1:15-16).

> I thank my God in all my remembrance of you, always offering prayer (Philippians 1:3-4).

> We give thanks to God, the Father of our Lord Jesus Christ, praying always for you (Colossians 1:3).

> We give thanks to God always for all of you, making mention of you in our prayers (1 Thessalonians 1:2).

> First of all, then, I urge that entreaties and prayers, petitions and thanksgivings, be made on behalf of all men (1 Timothy 2:1).

I thank God, whom I serve with a clear conscience the way my forefathers did, as I constantly remember you in my prayers night and day (2 Timothy 1:3).

I thank my God always, making mention of you in my prayers (Philemon 1:4).

It was exciting to discover how important our attitude is when we approach God in prayer, but it didn't answer my bigger question, which was "how do I pray in the Spirit?" With the connection between prayer and thanksgiving established in my mind, the Lord brought to my memory Psalm 95:

O come, let us sing for joy to the LORD, let us shout joyfully to the rock of our salvation. Let us come before His presence with thanksgiving. Let us shout joyfully to Him with psalms. For the LORD is a great God and a great King above all gods, in whose hands are the depths of the earth, the peaks of the mountains are His also. The sea is His, for it was He who made it, and His hands formed the dry land.

Come, let us worship and bow down, let us kneel before the LORD our Maker. For He is our God, and we are the people of His pasture and the sheep of His hand. Today, if you would hear His voice ... (verses 1-7).

Hearing God's Voice

We should come before His presence with thanksgiving because He is a great God and He has done great things for us. We were all destined for hell, but God has forgiven us and given us eternal life. That alone should cause us to be forever grateful. With that in mind, I saw the seven last words in the above passage: "Today, if you would hear His voice." I remember thinking, "Today I would love to hear Your voice!" Maybe I wasn't hearing His voice because I wasn't coming before His presence with thanksgiving. Then again, maybe I wasn't hearing His voice because I wasn't really listening.

Many people in the Old Testament discovered the hard way that complaining does not bring God's blessings. In Psalm 95:7, the word hear is the Hebrew word *shema*, which means to "hear as to obey." Verse eight continues with the clincher, "Do not harden your hearts." Why would that admonishment follow? I turned to Hebrews 4:7 which quotes Psalm 95, and read again, "Today if you hear His voice, do not harden your hearts." Hebrews 4 gives instruction concerning the "Sabbath rest" that remains. It is an exhortation to cease trusting in our own works and begin to trust in God's works.

Resting in the finished work of Christ did not typify my prayer life. Praying "in the name of Jesus" was just a phrase I tagged onto the end of my self-originated prayers. I confessed to God that my prayer time was mostly a work of the flesh and that I didn't always come before Him with an attitude of praise and thanksgiving.

God-Directed Prayer

The Lord had a lot more for me that night. I turned to Romans 8:26-27: "In the same way the Spirit also helps our weakness; for we do not know how to pray as we should, but the Spirit Himself intercedes for us with groanings too deep for words; and He who searches the hearts knows what the mind of the Spirit is, because He intercedes for the saints according to the will of God." Apart from God we really don't know how to pray or what to pray for, but the Holy Spirit does, and He will help us in our weakness. "Help" (*sunantilambano*) is a fascinating word. It has two prefixes in front of a word that is often translated as take. The Holy Spirit comes alongside us, bears us up, and takes us over to the other side (spiritually). The Holy Spirit is our connection with God. He intercedes for us on our behalf. The prayer that the Holy Spirit prompts us to pray is the prayer that God the Father will always answer.

How does the Holy Spirit help us in our weakness? I wasn't sure, but I tried something that evening. I prayed, "Okay, Lord – I'm setting aside my list, and I'm going to assume that whatever comes to my mind during this time of prayer is from You or is allowed by You. I'm going to let You lead my time of prayer." Whatever came to my mind that evening was what I prayed about. If it was a tempting thought, I talked to God about that area of weakness. If the busyness of the day clamored for my attention, I discussed that with God. I actively dealt with whatever came to my mind.

I wasn't passively letting thoughts control me. I put up the shield of faith, which stands against Satan's flaming arrows, and I was actively "taking every thought captive to the obedience of Christ" (2 Corinthians 10:5). If you don't assume responsibility for your thoughts, you may end up paying attention to a deceiving spirit.

If my thoughts weren't true or if they were evil (blasphemous, deceiving, accusing, or tempting), I chose not to believe them. I brought those thoughts to the Lord and exposed them to the light of His Word. In one sense, it doesn't make any difference whether our thoughts come from an external source, or from our memories, or from a deceiving spirit – we are responsible to take every thought captive to the obedience of Christ. That meant, if my thoughts were coming from Satan, God was allowing it. In my experience, this typically identifies an area of weakness or sin that I have not previously been honest with God about. In fact, God may allow us to get buffeted around by Satan until we bring our struggles before Him, the only One who can resolve them.

Don't Harden Your Heart

The truth is, I was hearing from God, but probably not what I wanted to hear. I started to realize why we were warned not to harden our hearts. If we don't harden our hearts, we will discover how personal our God really is. In the past, I would try to shove evil thoughts away without much success. But when I began to bring them to the light, I was amazed at how liberating that was. All the issues I had been trying to ignore during prayer were issues God wanted me to deal with. He wanted to make me aware of matters that were affecting our relationship. Now when I have tempting or accusing thoughts, I share them honestly with God and don't try to hide my human frailty.

When a thought that's hard to face comes into your mind, you will be tempted to change the subject and go back to your old prayer list. But why do you think God is allowing you to struggle with those thoughts? There may be many personal issues that we feel uncomfortable sharing with God, but that is part of the deception. After all, God already knows our thoughts (see Hebrews 4:12-13), and we are already forgiven, so why not be honest with Him? If God were to prioritize our prayer list, He would begin with personal issues that affect our relationship with Him.

Suppose you are a parent who has a rebellious child, and there are several issues that need to be resolved between the two of you that are keeping you from having an intimate relationship. That same child is always coming to you with a list of requests that will satisfy the child's desires. As you listen to the child's petitions, what is on your mind as a loving parent? Satisfying children's desires and granting their requests would only spoil them and not be good for their maturation. As a mature adult, you want to share with your children what is best for them, but what if they don't want to listen to you? What do you do? What does your Heavenly Father do?

Two members of the Trinity are actively participating with God's children in prayer all the time. The Holy Spirit helps them in their weaknesses, and Jesus "always lives to make intercession for them" (Hebrews 7:25). We can quench the Spirit (1 Thessalonians 5:19), and grieve Him by our actions (Ephesians 4:30), but why would we want to do that? The only impediment to effective prayer is us.

Take A Walk with God

After explaining this to my seminary students, I directed them to take a walk around the campus with God for the remainder of the class period. That would give them about forty-five minutes, which was far more time than most of them would spend on their daily devotions. I encouraged them to start by thanking God for all He had done for them. I encouraged them to deal honestly with any issues that came to their minds. If nothing came to mind, I suggested that they reflect upon God's goodness and thank Him for what He had done for them.

Many students returned with great stories. Some said they had accomplished more in those forty-five minutes than they ever had before in prayer. Some dealt with personal issues that they had never previously discussed with God. One Asian student said he knew for the first time that God was calling him to minister in China. Almost all found it to be a refreshing encounter with their loving Heavenly Father.

Silence Can Be Awkward

For myself, I found peace just sitting in the presence of God. I didn't feel like I had to say anything or keep a one-sided conversation going. It was liberating to simply sit in peaceful silence. My prayer time didn't end when I went to work. I was learning to pray without ceasing and practice the presence of God. The omnipresent God was always with me, and I was becoming more aware of His presence.

Have you ever been alone with a stranger? Silence can be awkward. You feel obligated to say something. So, you mention the weather or the latest news and sports, but nothing personal. On the other hand, I could sit in the same room with my wife for hours and not feel obligated to talk. Or we could ride together in a car for hours and not say anything. We were comfortable in the presence of each other. How well you handle solitude is one way to determine your spiritual condition. Can you be still and know that He is God? Are you comfortable in His presence?

Communication doesn't take place when there is only one talking. It happens when both parties listen. Prayer may be more about listening than talking. If sitting silently before the Lord is awkward, then you may want to consider how intimate your relationship with God is.

Living In the Light

"If we walk in the light as He Himself is in the light, we have fellowship with one another, and the blood of Jesus His Son cleanses us from all our sin" (1 John 1:7). Walking in the light does not mean moral perfection, because the next verse reads, "If we say that we have no sin, we are deceiving ourselves" (v. 8). Rather, walking in the light is living in conscious moral agreement with God.

Mature Christians live a confessional life. Confession literally means to agree with God. We don't confess our sins to be forgiven. We are forgiven because Christ died for our sins on the cross. Therefore, we confess our sins to have an intimate relationship with God. What makes it possible to be this open with God about our present moral condition is the fact that we already are His forgiven children.

Being Honest with God

Why is it so difficult to be honest with God? He demonstrated His love for us when He sent Jesus to die in our place (Romans 5:8). His love and forgiveness are unconditional. However, God is our Father, and like any good parent, He doesn't appreciate grumbling, complaining children, especially since He sacrificed His only begotten Son for every one of us. He will not be interested in our prayer lists if we don't "Seek first His kingdom and His righteousness" (Matthew 6:32). He is not going to help us develop our own kingdoms when we are called to establish His kingdom. Someone said that prayer is not conquering God's reluctance but laying hold of God's willingness. It is not trying to communicate our will to God but discerning His will for our lives. Those who seek to build His kingdom, and come before His presence with thanksgiving, will find grace and mercy in time of need:

> ... for we do not have a high priest who cannot sympathize with our weaknesses, but one who has been tempted in all things as we are, yet without sin. Therefore, let us draw near with confidence to the throne of grace, so that we may receive mercy and may find grace to help in the time of need (Hebrews 4:15-16).

Let us draw near with a sincere heart in full assurance of faith, having our hearts sprinkled clean from an evil conscience (Hebrews 10:22).

The Natural Progression of Prayer

There are three levels of prayer, and they are related to our maturity and intimacy with God. The first level is petition. "Let your requests be made known to God (Philippians 4:6). "You do not have because you do not ask" (James 4:2). Usually, our petitions reflect people and things we care about. The Lord told us to pray, "Give us this day our daily bread" (Matthew 6:11). Such prayers remind us of our need to be dependent upon God. If it helps us to keep a list of daily prayer reminders, we should do so. Daily needs are not selfish desires. "You ask and do not receive, because you ask with wrong motives, so that you may spend it on your pleasures" (James 4:3). Motive is critical, and it is unlikely that God will respond to self-centered prayers.

If you don't see any immediate answers to your petitions, you will likely be tempted to think that you could accomplish more if you started doing something for the Lord. It can also become wearisome petitioning God when communication is only one way. Petitioning God when our hearts aren't in it leads to stagnant growth and little productivity.

Personal Prayer

The second level of prayer is personal and two-way. We have entered into a new dimension of spirituality when we are comfortable in His presence and don't feel obligated to talk. It is not only okay to remain silent in God's presence, but also necessary if you want to hear from Him. Realizing that I didn't have to keep talking while communing with God changed my prayer life. I could rest in His presence and listen. Setting aside special times for prayer and devotion is important, and it should set us up for a Spirit-filled walk for the rest of the day.

The third level of prayer is intercessory. Most of what people call intercessory prayer today is little more than a petition. True intercessors have resolved their personal and spiritual conflicts because they have heard from God and repented. They know how to pray and what to pray for, because they are filled with the Holy Spirit. True intercessory prayer warriors are godly, humble, and mature. They pray privately in their homes and often at night. When God wakes them up, they know who and what to pray for, and they stay in prayer until God releases them. If you make their work known publicly and put them in the spotlight, you will likely undermine their ministry. Jesus said in Matthew 6:5-8:

> When you pray, you are not to be like the hypocrites; for they love to stand and pray in the synagogues and on the street corners so that they may be seen by men. Truly I say to you, they have their reward in full. But you, when you pray, go into your inner room, close your door and pray to your Father who is in secret, and your Father who sees what is done in secret will reward you. And when you are praying, do not use meaningless repetition as the gentiles do, for they suppose that they will be heard by their many words. So do not be like them; for your Father knows what you need before you ask Him.

Prayer and Praise

Praise and thanksgiving should be a part of every level of prayer. To come before God with thanksgiving is no different than coming before our earthly parents with an attitude of gratitude. It is upsetting to a parent when their children are always demanding, forever complaining, and never satisfied. How would you feel if you've given as much as you can as a parent and your child still wants more, and more, and more? On the other hand, how would you feel toward a child who respectfully says, "Thank you for being who you are. I love you and I know you're doing the best you can for me, and have my best interest at heart?"

Worship is ascribing to God His divine attributes. We are praising God when we declare them. Come before His presence with the understanding that God is our ever-present, all-powerful, all-knowing, and loving Heavenly Father. God doesn't need us to tell Him who He is and praising Him is not a bribe. It is actually for our benefit that we keep His divine attributes constantly in our minds. We don't have to petition God to be with us, or to be with our missionaries, because God is omnipresent. Scripture assures us that He will be with us to the ends of the earth. He will neither leave us nor forsake us. We need to be with Him and desire to be conscious of His presence.

Choosing Truth, Dispelling Darkness

The three levels of prayer correlate with the three levels of growth depicted in 1 John 2:12-14. Little children are those whose sins are forgiven. They have overcome the penalty of their sins by the grace of God, and they petition God for daily needs. Old people that have a deep reverential knowledge of God intercede on behalf of others. The "young men" are those who "have overcome the evil one." They can pray more effectively because they can hear from God.

Learning to overcome the evil one is essential for our mental peace. It is impossible to be led by the Holy Spirit if you are paying attention to an evil spirit. Tempting, accusing, and deceiving thoughts are distracting. If you are plagued by tempting thoughts, bring the basis for the temptation before God and seek to resolve any personal and spiritual conflicts that are keeping you from having an intimate relationship with Him. That is what we hope to accomplish by leading people through *The Steps to Freedom in Christ.* "I shall wash my hands in innocence, and I will go about Your altar, O LORD, that I may proclaim with the voice of thanksgiving, and declare all Your wonders. O LORD, I love the habitation of Your house and the place where Your glory dwells" (Psalm 26: 6-8).

Such was the case for the thirteen-year veteran missionary who wrote me the following:

> "I have been wanting to write to you for a while, but I've waited this long to confirm to myself that this is truly "for reals," as my five-year-old daughter says. I want to share an entry from my journal that I wrote two days after our meeting. Since Friday afternoon I have felt like a different person. The fits of rage and anger are gone. My spirit is so calm and full of joy. I wake up singing praise to God in my heart. That edge of tension and irritation is gone. I feel so free. The Bible has been really exciting, stimulating, and more understandable than ever before. There was nothing "dramatic" that happened during our session, yet I know in the deepest part of my being that something has changed. I am no longer bound by accusations, doubts, and thoughts

of suicide, murder, or other harm that came straight from hell into my head. There is a serenity in my mind and spirit, a daily consciousness that is profound.

I've been set free!

I'm excited and expectant about my future now. I know that I will be growing spiritually again, and I look forward happily to the discovery of the person God created and redeemed, as well as the transformation of my marriage. It is so wonderful to have joy after so long of a darkness.

It's been two and a half months since I wrote that, and I'm firmly convinced of the significant benefits of your ministry. I had been in therapy for several months and I was making some progress, but there is no comparison with the steps I'm able to make now. My ability to "process" things has increased many-fold. Not only is my spirit more serene, but my head is also actually clearer. It's easier to make connections and integrate things now. It seems like everything is easier to understand now.

My relationship with God has changed significantly. For eight years I felt that He was distant from me. Shortly before I met you, I was desperately crying out to God to be set free, to release me from the bondage I was in. I wanted so badly to meet with Him again, to know His presence was with me again. I needed to know Him as a friend, as a companion, not as the distant authority figure He had become in my mind. Since that day, two and half months ago, I've seen my trust in Him grow. I've seen my ability to be honest with Him increase. I really have been experiencing that spiritual growth I'd anticipate in my journal entry. It's great!"

Discussion Questions

1. Have you experienced the same difficulties in prayer as the author?
2. Why is our attitude so important when communicating with God?
3. Why shouldn't we harden our hearts when hearing from God?
4. How does the Holy Spirit enable us to pray?
5. How is a child's relationship with a parent similar to your relationship with God?
6. Do you have a quiet and peaceful mind when you sit in silence before God?
7. What does it mean to live in the light?
8. Why is it so important to be honest with God?
9. What is the difference between petitioning God and intercessory prayer?
10. What does it mean to praise God and how does doing so relate to prayer?

Chapter Nine: Walking by the Spirit

Yet it seems to me that here he has pronounced a great and remarkable eulogy on the law. For the power of the law was such as to put it in the place of the office of the Spirit before the Spirit came to us. That is not to say that one should therefore cleave to this custodian. For then we were properly under the law, so that by fear we might restrain our desires, the Spirit not yet having appeared. But what need is there now of the law when the Spirit has been given? This grace does not merely bid us to restrain from the commands of the Old Covenant, but also quenches them and leads us on to a higher rule of life.[34]

Chrysostom, Homily on Galatians 5:18

A young pilot had just passed the point of no return when the weather changed for the worse. Visibility dropped to a matter of feet as the clouds descended upon the earth. Putting complete trust in the cockpit instruments was a new experience for him, for the ink was still wet on the certificate verifying that he was qualified for instrument flying.

It was the landing that worried him the most. His destination was a crowded metropolitan airport that he wasn't familiar with. In a few minutes he would be in radio contact with the tower. Until then, he was alone with his thoughts. Flying with no visibility, he became aware of how easy it would be to panic. Twice he reached for the radio to broadcast, "Mayday!" Instead, he forced himself to go over and over the words of his instructor who required him to memorize the instruction manual. He didn't care for it at the time, but now he was thankful.

Finally, he heard the voice of the air traffic controller. Trying not to sound apprehensive, the young pilot asked for landing instructions. "I'm going to put you on a holding pattern," the controller responded. Great, thought the pilot! He knew that his safe landing was in the hands of this person. He had to draw upon previous flight instruction and trust the voice of an air traffic controller he couldn't see. The words of an old hymn, "Trust and obey for there's no other way," took on a new meaning. Aware that this was no time for pride, he informed the controller, "This is not a seasoned pro up here. I would appreciate any help you could give me." "You got it!" he heard back.

For the next forty-five minutes, the controller gently guided the pilot through the blinding fog. As course and altitude corrections came periodically, the young pilot realized the controller was guiding him around obstacles and away from potential collisions. With the words of the instruction book in his mind, and with the gentle voice of the controller, he landed safely.

The Holy Spirit guides us through the maze of life much like that air traffic controller. The controller assumed that the young pilot understood the instructions in the flight manual. His guidance was based on that. Such is the case with the Holy Spirit; He can guide us only to the extent that we have the knowledge of God's Word and His ways established in our minds.

We need God's guidance to survive the difficult days that lie ahead. Living by the law has never worked, and neither does tolerating sin. Neither legalism nor license can stem the tide of moral decay. The balanced answer we need is given in Galatians 5:16-18:

> But I say, walk by the Spirit, and you will not carry out the desires of the flesh. For the flesh sets its desire against the Spirit and the Spirit against the flesh. For these are in opposition to one another, so that you may not do the things that you please. But if you are led by the Spirit, you are not under the law.

How do we walk or live by the Spirit? If I answered the question by giving you three steps and a formula, I'd be putting you back under the law. Air traffic controllers are living people, not previously recorded voices based on consistent weather conditions assuming no other planes in the air. The Holy Spirit is not an "it"; the Holy Spirit is God. The above passage explains more what walking by the Spirit is not, rather than what it is. But that is helpful since it provides parameters within which we can live liberated lives in Christ.

Walking By the Spirit Is Not License

Many conservative churches in the first half of the twentieth century endured a lot of hellfire and damnation messages. The Vietnamese War in the 1960s and political unrest ushered in a Cultural Revolution that espoused free sex and drugs. There was also a spiritual renewal at the time such as the Jesus People and charismatic movements that brought new life to many churches. In some churches, the pendulum was swinging from legalism to license. They reasoned, "Since I am under the grace of God, I can do whatever I want. Just flow by the Spirit. A God of love wouldn't send me to hell." But Paul is teaching just the opposite. If we walk by the Spirit, we won't carry out the desires of the flesh and won't do whatever we please.

Walking by the Spirit is not a license. License is defined as an excessive or undisciplined lifestyle constituting the abuse of a privilege. To be licentious means that one lacks moral discipline and has little to no regard for accepted rules and regulations. If there were no moral restraints and no boundaries to govern our behavior, we would all slide into moral decadence. Imagine the air traffic controller saying to the pilot, "You have my permission to land any time and any place you want." That pilot would probably crash and burn!

The Apostle Paul wrote, "You were called to freedom, brethren, only do not turn your freedom into an opportunity for the flesh, but through love serve one another" (Galatians 5:13). We have been set free by the grace of God to live a responsible life.

Many people confuse license with freedom. True freedom doesn't just lie in the exercise of choices, but in the consequences of the choices as well. You have the "freedom" to tell a lie, but you would be in bondage to that lie. You would have to remember the nature of the lie and to whom you told it. You may choose to rob a bank, but you will always be looking over your shoulder, fearing you may be caught. License leads to bondage.

If we choose to walk by the flesh, we will have to live with the negative consequences stemming from the choices we make. Free sex isn't free. The cost of human lives alone is staggering, and roughly half the adult population has sexually transmitted diseases. The pro-choice movement wants to eliminate the consequences of their choices by killing babies. They had a choice to have or not have sex. We don't have an abortion problem. We have an irresponsible sex problem.

Walking By the Spirit Is Not Legalism

Walking by the Spirit is not legalism: "If you are led by the Spirit, you are not under the law" (Galatians 5:16). If you believe that laying down the law is the answer, then you need to know what Scripture says about that. First, the law will function as a curse (Galatians 3:10-14, NIV):

> All who rely on observing the law are under a curse, for it is written: "Cursed is everyone who does not continue to do everything written in the Book of the Law." Clearly, no one is justified before God by the law, because "The righteous will live by faith." The law is not based on faith; on the contrary, "The man who does these things will live by them." Christ redeemed us from the curse of the law by becoming a curse for us, for it is written: "Cursed is everyone who is hung on a tree." He redeemed us in order that the blessing given to Abraham might come to the Gentiles through Christ Jesus, so that by faith we might receive the promise of the Spirit.

Legalists are a pain in the neck to themselves and others. They are driven by guilt, and no matter how hard they try, perfection eludes them. "For whoever keeps the whole law and yet stumbles on one point, he has become guilty of all" (James 2:10). We are not saved by how we perform, but by what we believe. "For the law has become our tutor to lead us to Christ that we may be justified by faith" (Galatians 3:24).

"This is the only thing I want to find out about you: did you receive the Spirit by the works of the law, or by hearing with faith? Are you so foolish? Having begun by the Spirit, are you now being perfected by the flesh" (Galatians 3:2,3)? We are saved by faith, and we are sanctified by faith. If we want to change people's behavior, we have to change what they believe, not what they do. We are transformed by the renewing of our minds, not by the renewing of our behavior. How we live is just a reflection of what we have chosen to believe. "Even so faith, if it has no works, is dead, being by itself. But someone may well say, 'You have faith and I have works; show me your faith without works, and I will show you my faith by my works'" (James 2:17,18). In other words, if what you believe doesn't affect your walk and your talk, then you don't really believe.

The second limitation of the law is that it is powerless to give life. Telling people that what they are doing is wrong does not give them the power to stop. "Is the law then contrary to the promises of God? May it never be! For if a law had been given which was able to impart life, then righteousness would indeed have been based on the law (Galatians 3:21). Remember that life means that our souls are in union with God. We were dead in our trespasses and sins, but now we are alive in Christ: "We are servants of a new covenant, not of the letter, but of the Spirit. For the letter kills, but the Spirit gives life" (2 Corinthians 3:6).

The futility of trying to live according to the law was illustrated on the front page of a major city's newspaper. A school official was commissioned by the state to teach students how to practice safe sex. It wasn't a Christian program, but part of the instruction was to exercise moral restraint. The instructor admitted that she had a major weight problem and that she had read many books on nutrition, exercise, and diet. She could also give a lecture on those subjects, but even though she possessed that knowledge, it didn't stop her that day from having a second piece of pie.

Her admission in the paper was not only honest, but it was also insightful. She was supposed to be a mature adult and more than twice the age of the students, but knowledge about the rights and wrongs of eating didn't curb her appetites. So how could she expect students less mature than herself to follow her instructions? Good point!

No Longer Slaves to Sin

The law has a third limitation: It has the capacity to stimulate the desire to do what it was intended to prohibit. The law can actually arouse our sinful passions. "For while we were in the flesh, the sinful passions, which were aroused by the law, were at work in the members of our body to bear fruit for death" (Romans 7:5). Is the law then sinful? Not according to Romans 7:7,8:

> What shall we say then? Is the law sin? May it never be! On the contrary, I would not have come to know sin except through the law; for I would not have known about coveting if the law had not said, "You shall not covet." But sin, taking opportunity through the commandment, produced in me coveting of every kind; for apart from the law sin is dead.

If you don't believe that laying down the law doesn't stimulate the desire to do otherwise, then try telling your children they can go one place but not another. The moment you say that, where do they want to go? The forbidden fruit will seem to be the most desirable, as was the case with Eve. A church posted a list of movies the students couldn't see, which quickly became a list of movies they wanted to see. Those were the "good" movies! The youth actually copied the list off the wall of the church and shared it with their friends.

Of course, we need a moral standard, for without it we wouldn't come to Christ. But now that we are alive in Christ, the law is no longer the means by which we live a righteous life. Christ as the fulfillment of the law brings the believer into a new relationship with the law. As believers "in Christ" we are no longer under the law (Romans 6:14,15; Galatians 3:23-25; 5:18). We are free from the law (Galatians 4:8-10; 5:1-3; Colossians 2:20) in two significant ways:

Free from Legal Bondage

Under the Old Covenant, violators of the law are deserving of punishment. Because everyone has broken the law, we were all under the judgment of death. "In Christ," however, we are viewed as having died to the law through His sacrificial death for us and are thus "released from the law" (Romans 7:6). "Christ redeemed us from the curse of the law by becoming a curse for us" (Galatians 3:13). Believers have fully met the requirements of the law in terms of law-breaking, because we have been identified with Christ in His death (Romans 6:5).

In addition, because we have been identified with Christ's resurrection, we stand in His righteousness (His perfect obedience), so that the law can no longer condemn us in the future. We have "become the righteousness of God" in Christ; He is our "righteousness" (1 Corinthians 1:30). The law of the spirit of life in Christ Jesus has set us free from the law of sin and the law of death (Romans 8:2). Physical death is still imminent, and sin is still present and appealing. Since we have eternal life in Christ Jesus, we need not fear physical death. The Apostle Paul wrote, "For to me, to live is Christ and to die is gain" (Philippians 1:21).

The law of sin and death is still present, because you cannot do away with law. But you can overcome a law by a greater law, which is the "law of life in Christ Jesus." None of us can fly in our own strength, because of the law of gravity. But we can fly "in" an airplane because there is a greater power in the airplane than the law of gravity. If you think the law of gravity is no longer effective, then flip the switch at 20,000 feet. You will crash and burn. If you live by faith according to what God says is true in the power of the Holy Spirit, you will not carry out the desire of the flesh. That is how we live a righteous life "in" Christ.

Free from the Legal Requirement

Believers are free from the law as a "supervisory custodian" of our lives. "The law has become our tutor to lead us to Christ, that we may be justified by faith. But now that faith has come, we are no longer under the law" (Galatians 3:24,25). "The word, tutor, which suggests a teaching function, is the Greek word *paidagogos*. A *paidagogos* was usually a slave who was charged with the supervision and conduct of one or more sons in the ancient patrician household. He did no formal teaching but administered the directives of the father in a custodial manner. His supervision and discipline did, however, contribute to the instruction."[35]

The Apostle uses the word paidagogos to point out that the law served a supervisory control over God's people for a limited time, i.e., until Christ came, which he goes on to explain in Galatians 4:1-5:

> What I am saying is that as long as the heir is a child... he is subject to guardians and trustees until the time set by his father. So also, when we were children, we were in slavery under the basic principles of the world. But when the time had fully come, God sent His Son, born of a woman, born under the law, to redeem those under the law, that we might receive the full rights of sons.

Prior to Christ's coming, God's people were like children under a tutor. But with Christ's sacrificial death and resurrection completed and the sending of the Holy Spirit, believers are now "adult sons" and no longer under the "tutor" of the law. Control is no longer from without, but from within. Self-control is a fruit of the Spirit.

Think of the Christian walk as a journey up a mountain road. The Holy Spirit provides guidance and protection for those who walk the narrow path. To the right of the path is a cliff. It is too steep to climb down and too far to jump. It is a tempting choice, however. You could sail off that cliff and enjoy an exhilarating "flight." But that choice has serious consequences – like the sudden stop at the end! Succumbing to the desires of the flesh, doing as you please, and demanding your "right" to freedom of choice without considering the consequences is license. It's a deadly step in the wrong direction.

To the left of that road is a roaring fire. The accuser of the brethren has a field day with those who choose to deviate from the narrow path by living under the law. "It was for freedom that Christ set us free; therefore, keep standing firm and do not be subject again to a yoke of slavery. Behold I, Paul, say to you that if you receive circumcision, Christ will be of no benefit to you" (Galatians 5:1). In other words, don't go back to the law.

The devil is a tempter. He wants us to jump off that cliff. "Go on and do it. Everybody is doing it. You will get away with it. Who would know? You know you want to." As soon as you give in to the temptation, his role changes from tempter to accuser. "You're sick. And you call yourself a Christian. You will never get away with this. God can't possibly love such a miserable failure as you."

So, if walking by the Spirit is not license, and it's not legalism, then what is it? It is liberty: "Now the Lord is a Spirit, and where the Spirit of the Lord is there is liberty" (2 Corinthians 3:17).

Walking with God

Living by the Spirit also has two parameters to keep in mind. First, walking by the Spirit is not sitting passively expecting God to do everything for us. Second, walking by the Spirit is not running around in endless activities as though everything depended upon us. How much is accomplished in the kingdom of God if we expect God to do everything for us? Nothing! It is the eternal purpose of God to make His wisdom known through the Church. (Ephesians 3:8-11). On the other hand, how much gets accomplished for the kingdom of God if we try to do it all by ourselves? Jesus said, "Apart from me you can do nothing" (John 15:5).

There was a pastor whose favorite hobby was gardening. One of his deacons commented, "The Lord sure gave you a beautiful garden." The pastor responded, "You should have seen it when the Lord had it all by Himself." We have the privilege to water and plant, but God causes the increase. If there is no watering or planting, then nothing grows either.

Jesus said, "Come to me all who are weary and heavy-laden, and I will give you rest. Take My yoke upon you and learn from me, for I am gentle and humble in heart, and you shall find rest for your souls. For my yoke is easy and my load is light" (Matthew 11:28-30). Jesus was a carpenter in His youth, but carpenters didn't frame houses as we do today. They fashioned yokes and doors, which Jesus would use metaphorically of Himself.

A yoke harnessed two oxen together. After much training, the lead ox knew how to walk. If he kept a steady even pace, he wouldn't burn out before noon. He also learned to look neither to the left nor to the right. When yoked with another ox, they learned to pull together. It was the only way they were going to accomplish anything.

For the purpose of training, young oxen are paired together with an old, seasoned ox who knows how to walk. One young ox got impatient with the slow pace and wanted to run ahead. It got a sore neck. Another young ox felt like doing nothing and just sat. It too got a sore neck. The lead ox is going to keep right on walking, no matter what the young ox does, because he is listening to his master. So, if you are burned out or have dropped out, consider being yoked with Jesus. His ways aren't hard, and you will find rest, because He will maintain a steady pace right down the center of the narrow way.

When my children were little, we had a perfect family dog. When little Missy died, it was traumatic for all of us. I hurried to a pet store the same day and bought a replacement dog. This is a "marriage on the rebound" story. Buster grew up to be a Dawg! He was a neurotic mess. I signed him up for twelve lessons at a dog obedience school and sent my son off with Buster and a choke chain. After two weeks my son gave up.

One day I decided to give Buster a lesson on how to walk with his master. So, I put a choke chain around his neck, and we went for a walk. I was the master, and I knew where I wanted to walk. That dumb dog nearly choked himself to death trying to run. When Buster stopped to sniff a flower or some gross thing, I kept on walking, and the walk became a drag. I was determined to teach that dog how to walk by his master. Then he would stray off the path and end up winding his leash around a tree. The result was like a wild ride at an amusement park as I kept on walking. You ask, "Did that dumb dog ever learn to walk obediently by his master?" No, he never did. I've known a few Christians who haven't either.

Jesus said, "Take My yoke upon you." The flesh responds, "That's all I need is another yoke!" But you can't put on the yoke of Christ without throwing off the yokes of legalism and license. Jesus may be our crutch, but He is the only one we need. "Learn from Me," Jesus said. We would learn to take one day at a time. We would learn the priority of relationships. We would learn that our walk is one of faith, not sight; one of grace, and not legalism.

Jesus said, "My yoke is easy, and my load is light." If we find ourselves huffing and puffing our way through life, maybe we're not walking with God. Maybe we're living according to the flesh. You don't evaluate your spiritual progress by saying, "We did this, and we did that. We went here and we went there." We don't measure our spirituality by our activities; we measure it by how much fruit remains.

Matthew 11:28-30 is the only place in the New Testament where Jesus described himself. He said, "I am gentle and humble in heart." We have been invited to walk with the gentle Jesus. Imagine that! "As you, therefore, have received Christ Jesus, so walk in him (Colossians 2:6).

Following Our Guide

Being led by the Spirit also has two parameters. First, the Holy Spirit is not pushing us. There is a major difference between being called into ministry and being driven to perform. The latter leads to burnout. If you are being pressured to make a hasty decision, just say "no." God doesn't lead that way. The devil does. He demands an answer right now and withdraws the offer if time for consideration is requested. The guidance of God may come suddenly, but it never comes to the spiritually unprepared. Pentecost was sudden, but the disciples had spent days in prayerful preparation.

Second, we are not being lured away in some secretive and clandestine way. God does everything in the light. Those who are easily lured away have no spiritual discipline or discernment. They don't study, and they don't pray. They want the air traffic controller to explain the instruction manual to them while they are in the air.

I had the joy of raising sheep on the family farm. However, I can tell you from experience that sheep are not the smartest animals on the farm. They rank right up there with chickens. For instance, you can self-feed cattle and pigs, but you can't self-feed sheep. If left alone to graze in lush green pastures without a shepherd, they will literally eat themselves to death. That is why the Shepherd, "Makes me lie down in green pastures" (Psalm 23:2).

I grew up driving the sheep from the rear, much like an Australian sheepdog. However, that is not the case in Israel. In my trips to the Holy Land, I observed shepherds sitting patiently while the flock fed on the grass. When an area was sufficiently grazed, the shepherd would say something and walk off. The sheep looked up and followed him. What a beautiful illustration of what the Lord said in John 10:27, "My sheep hear my voice, and I know them, and they follow me."

Walking by the Spirit is neither legalism nor license. It's not sitting passively, waiting for God to do something, nor is it running around in endless activities trying to accomplish everything by our own strength and resources. If we walk by the Spirit, we are neither driven nor lured off the path of faith. "For all who are being led by the Spirit of God, these are the sons of God" (Romans 8:14).

Discussion Questions

1. How is the guidance of God similar to the guidance of an air traffic controller?
2. Why is trying to live by the law insufficient?
3. What is the difference between freedom and license?
4. Summarize the three limitations of the law?
5. How do you overcome the law of sin and death?
6. How does the Holy Spirit replace the law as our tutor?
7. What is Satan's role when we deviate from the narrow path of righteous living?
8. What is wrong with sitting around passively in holy piety and running around in endless activities?
9. What did Jesus mean when He said, "take my yoke upon you?"
10. How are we like sheep?

Chapter Ten: Intimacy with God

He is LORD, because He rules over the universe. He is Father because He is before all things. He is Fashioner and Creator, because He is Creator and Maker of the universe. He is the highest, because He is above all. He is Almighty, because He Himself rules and embraces everything. The heights of heaven and the depths of the abysses, as well as the ends of the earth.[36]

Theophilus (c. 180)

If anybody could qualify to have a relationship with God on the basis of the Old Covenant and Jewish heritage, it would be the Apostle Paul. He was a "Hebrew of Hebrews" (Philippians 3:5) and "as to righteousness which is in the law, found blameless" (v. 6). The apostle was a zealous defender of the faith and knew all about God, but until the Lord struck him down on the Damascus Road, he didn't know Him at all. He had an Old Covenant relationship with God, but not a personal one. His conversion cost him everything he had worked for. He lost his social status, his friends, his reputation, his position in the synagogue, and his respect in the Jewish community. But to Paul that was all rubbish compared to knowing Christ Jesus his Lord (v. 8).

According to The Westminster Shorter Catechism[37], "God is a Spirit, infinite, eternal, and unchangeable in His being, wisdom, power, holiness, justice, goodness and truth." That helps us to know about God, but can we actually know God? Personally? God is incomprehensible according to Scripture: "How great is God – beyond understanding! The number of His years is past finding out" (Job 36:26). We cannot fully comprehend the Infinite One, yet we can know Him as our Heavenly Father. Paul prayed, "that the God of our Lord Jesus Christ, the glorious Father, may give you the spirit of wisdom and revelation, so that you may know Him better" (Ephesians 1:17 NIV).

God has made Himself known to us through His Word, but the written Word by itself can only give us knowledge about God. The ultimate revelation of God is Jesus who said, "He who has seen me has seen the Father" (John 14:9). It is through the living Word that we personally know our Heavenly Father: "No one knows the Son except the Father, and no one knows the Father except the Son and those to whom the Son chooses to reveal Him" (Matthew 11:27).

Outer Level of Intimacy with God

Having a personal relationship with God means that we are spiritually alive and can have fellowship with Him. That being the case, stop reading for a moment and reflect on your own personal relationship with God. How close are you to your Heavenly Father? You are at this very moment as intimate with God as you have chosen to be. To help you assess that I am going to describe four levels of intimacy with God and start with those who are furthest from Him.

In Exodus 19:3:

> Moses went up to God, and the Lord called to Him from the mountain saying, 'Thus you shall say to the house of Jacob and tell the sons of Israel.

What follows in the text is the Mosaic covenant, which was conditional (vs. 5,6):

> Now then, if you will indeed obey my voice and keep my commandments, then you shall be my own possession among all the peoples, for all the earth is mine; and you shall be to me a kingdom of priests and a holy nation. These are the words that you shall speak to the sons of Israel.

> Moses shared what he heard, and the people said, "All that the Lord has spoken we will do" (v. 8).

Give them credit for their desire to be obedient. Moses gathered all the people who were to consecrate themselves. On the third day, the Lord would come down on Mount Sinai in the sight of all the people. Moses was also instructed to set bounds for them. They were not to go up on the mountain or touch the border of it lest they die:

> And Moses brought the people out of the camp to meet God, and they stood at the foot of the mountain. Now Mount Sinai was all in smoke because the Lord descended upon it in fire, and its smoke ascended like the smoke of a furnace, and the whole mountain quaked violently. When the sound of the trumpet grew louder and louder, Moses spoke, and God answered him with thunder (vs. 17-19).

There were no atheists in the camp that day, but why the boundary? The answer is explained in Exodus 20:18-20:

> All the people perceived the thunder and the lightning flashes and the sound of the trumpet and the mountain smoking; and when the people saw it, they trembled and stood at a distance. Then they said to Moses, "Speak to us

yourself and we will listen; but let not God speak to us, or we will die." Moses said to the people, "Do not be afraid for God has come to test you, and in order that the fear of him may remain with you, so that you may not sin."

It was a test, and it revealed two characteristics about those who occupy the outer level of intimacy. First, their orientation toward God was to avoid punishment, i.e., to avoid hell. They have their fire insurance and that is all they want. So, they go on living the natural life with little interest in pursuing their relationship with God. They check in on most Sundays to be sure their insurance policy is still good.

Second, they settle for a second-hand relationship or experience with God. They wanted Moses to speak to God for them and they would hear from God through Moses. That is like saying today, "Pastor would you pray for me, and study for me? Let me know what God says on Sunday morning." How sad is that? Maybe the real tragedy is the pastors who are willing to settle for that and keep preaching salvation messages. Those who want an intimate relationship with God will start looking elsewhere, and those who stay are the ones unsure of their salvation or who fear that leaving will seal their fate (avoiding punishment).

When I was in the eighth grade our school had a program called "religious day instruction." Every Tuesday afternoon they shortened the classes so we could go to the church of our choice for the last hour. It wasn't forced religion. Students could go to the study hall if they wanted. I chose to go to the church of my mother's choice! One nice fall afternoon I skipped religious day instruction and played in the nearby park. I came back to the school in time to catch the bus. I thought I got away with it.

I did not. The principal called me into his office the next day and chewed me out. He finished his lecture by saying, "I have arranged for you to be off Thursday and Friday from school." Was I expelled from school for two days for skipping religious day instruction? I was shocked and I was not looking forward to going home and sharing that news with my parents. I had alternative thoughts while riding the school bus like, "Get up tomorrow and pretend that you are sick for two days." Or "Do your chores and pretend that you got on the bus and then go hide in the woods for the rest of the day." I didn't think I could pull either one off, so I chose to take my medicine, but I was not looking forward to seeing my authority figures.

I confessed to my mother because I thought there would be some mercy there. "Mom," I said, "I got expelled from school for two days because I skipped religious day instruction." She responded with a surprised look and said, "What?" Then her expression changed, and she said, "Oh, Neil, I forget to tell you. We called the school yesterday to ask if you could be off for two days to help us pick corn." Incredible. I could have gotten away with my indiscretion, but God arranged it so that there would be no secrets between myself and my parents.

Had I known that my absence on Thursday and Friday was already excused, would I have dreaded going home? Hardly! I would probably have run up the lane and gladly sought out my parents. The Apostle Paul said, "Therefore, having been justified by faith, we have peace with God through our Lord Jesus Christ" (Romans 5:1). If you knew that, you would go running to your Heavenly Father. "There is no fear in love; but perfect love casts out fear, because fear involves punishment, and the one who fears is not perfected in love" (1 John 4:18).

Too many Christians live as though they are walking on glass and if they make one wrong move then the hammer of God will fall on them. Dear Christian, the hammer fell. It fell on Christ. We are not sinners in the hands of an angry God, we are saints in the hands of a loving God who is calling us to come to His presence with confidence and boldness (Ephesians 3:12).

Therefore, "Let us draw near with a sincere heart in full assurance of faith, having our hearts sprinkled clean from an evil conscience and our bodies washed with pure water" (Hebrews 10: 22).

The Second Level of Intimacy

> Then Moses went up with Aaron, Nadab and Abihu, and seventy of the elders of Israel, and they saw the God of Israel; and under His feet there appeared to be a pavement of sapphire, as clear as the sky itself. Yet he did not stretch out his hand against the nobles of the sons of Israel; and they saw God, and they ate and drank.

> *Exodus 24:9,10*

Notice how quickly the numbers fall off when you climb the mountain of God. The seventy-five saw only a manifestation of God because nobody living in a natural body can fully look upon God. We look forward to receiving a resurrected body and seeing God face to face, but that will only happen for us when we exchange the natural and perishable body for a spiritual and immortal body (1 Corinthians 15:53). They had a life-changing encounter with God, but seventy-three of them slid back down the mountain. They were told to wait while Moses and Joshua went further up the mountain, but they got tired of waiting. They walked back down the mountain and built themselves a golden calf.

Aaron instructed the people to tear off their gold jewelry, and with it, he made a molten calf and said, "This is your god, O Israel, who brought you up from the land of Egypt" (Exodus 32: 4). Impersonal gods don't have to be served.

Have you ever wondered why God doesn't settle once and for all the question of His existence? Why doesn't He show himself for who He is? Suppose He did provide scientific proof to the whole world that He exists. He could use some kind of mass communication to let everyone know that on a certain date and time, He would make himself known to everyone in a way that is indisputable. He would present Himself in a visible way so that the entire world could see Him in the clouds. Photographs would be taken of His appearance, and nobody could refute the evidence.

At first, the whole world would be astounded, and every television station would be showing pictures and hearing testimonies of those who saw God. Dramatic changes would probably be made initially, but it wouldn't be long before people would settle back into their old routines of work and play. Imagine a father showing his son a picture of God and saying, "Look son, God exists." To which the son replies, "So?" So, what difference does that make? Those on the second level of intimacy believe God exists, but they still rule their own lives.

In reality, everything should change the moment we enter into a relationship with God. God has taken up residence in our lives. Christ dwells in our hearts through faith (Ephesians 3:17). We have been given the Holy Spirit, and Jesus said, "He will glorify me, for He will take of mine and will disclose it to you. All things that the Father has are mine; therefore, I said that he takes of mine and will disclose it to you" (John 16:14,15). Assured of salvation we learn to walk by faith in the power of the Holy Spirit. We learn to accept one another just as Christ has accepted us (Romans 15:7). We learn to be merciful as God has been merciful to us, and to forgive others as we have been forgiven. We love because He first loved us. We stop going to work just to earn a living. At our places of employment, we start doing our work heartily as for the Lord rather than for men, because it is the Lord Christ whom we serve (Ephesians 3:23). We live openly in the presence of God which affects everything we do and say.

The Third Level of Intimacy

> Now the Lord said to Moses, "Come up to me on the mountain and remain there, and I will give you the stone tablets with the law and the commandments which I have written for their instruction. So, Moses arose with Joshua his servant, and Moses went up to the mountain of God.
>
> *Exodus 24:12,13*

Why Joshua? What was unique about Joshua that enabled him to take the next step up the mountain of God? After the golden calf debacle, Moses pitched a tent outside the camp of the Israelites and called it the tent of meeting (Exodus 33:7). Those who sought the Lord went to the tent. "When all the people saw the pillar of cloud standing at the entrance of the tent, all the people would arise and worship, each at the entrance of his tent. Thus, the Lord used to speak to Moses face to face, just as a man speaks to his friend. When Moses returned to the camp, his servant Joshua, the son of Nun, a young man, would not depart from the tent" (33:10,11).

Level two Christians fulfill their obligations to God and then go on about their business. Level three Christians don't want to depart from God. They have tasted the goodness of God and know that there is more to seek after. Having been a seminary professor, I have seen the difference in my students. Some came to fulfill the degree requirements to enable their "professional" journey. They were satisfied with just getting a diploma. A small number weren't satisfied with that. They would stay after class and ask questions. They wanted more than information. They wanted a deeper understanding of who they are in Christ, and who God is.

The Moses and Joshua relationship was much like Elijah and Elisha. God had directed Elijah to anoint Elisha as a prophet in his place (1 Kings. 19:16). The two were leaving Gilgal when "Elijah said to Elisha, 'Stay here please, for the Lord has sent me as far as Bethel'. But Elisha said, 'As the Lord lives and as you yourself live, I will not leave you.' So, they both went to Bethel" (2 Kings 2:2).

At Bethel there were the "sons of the prophets" who invited Elisha to stay with them since his master, Elijah, would be taken away from him that day. These "sons of the prophets" had made no name for themselves. They were living off the reputation of their fathers. This colorless conformity to the status quo may have offered Elisha job security, but that is not what he was looking for. He was seeking what Elijah had.

Then Elijah told Elisha to stay in Bethel while he went to Jericho, but that was not what Elisha was about to do. So, the two went to Jericho and there were more "sons of the prophets" who offered Elisha the same "opportunity" to stay with them, and Elijah encouraged Elisha to do so as he was going to the Jordan River. By now you should know what Elisha was going to do, and so the two went to the Jordan River, but this time the sons of the prophets followed them.

At the river, Elijah took off his mantle and struck the water, and the river parted. "The two of them crossed over on dry ground" (v. 8). Elijah then said to Elisha, 'Ask what I shall do for you before I am taken away from you'. And Elisha said, 'Please, let a double portion of your spirit be upon me'" (v. 9). He wasn't asking for twice as much. He was asking for the birthright, which was given to a firstborn son. Elijah told Elisha that he had asked for a hard thing, but it would be given to him if he saw Elijah taken from him that day. As they were walking and talking together, the chariots of God took Elijah to heaven in a whirlwind, and his mantle fell to the ground.

Elijah had just taken Elisha as far as one man can take another, which is the wrong side of the Jordan River. To further clarify the significance of that, recall that Jacob had labored on that side of the Jordan River after he ran from his father, Isaac. For twenty years he bargained for one wife and got another as he struggled to relate to his father-in-law. Fed up with it all, he finally picked up his two wives and livestock and headed for home to face his father and brother. At the Jordan River he sent his family and livestock across the river and that night he wrestled with the angel of the Lord (Genesis 32:24, see also Hosea 12:4). He struggled to get away from this pre-incarnate appearance of Christ. But at the crack of dawn, he looked into the face of pure love, and the struggle changed. Now he was holding on to this "man," asking for a blessing. The Lord touched the socket of his thigh so that he would know forever that this was no dream and asked him his name, and he said "Jacob." "Your name shall no longer be Jacob, but Israel; for you have striven with God and with men and have prevailed" (v. 28). Jacob named the place Peniel, which means the face of God. On the east side of the Jordan, he was Jacob, but when he limped across to the other side, he was Israel. He had discovered God for himself.

Now Elisha finds himself stranded on the wrong side of the Jordan. Elijah could have taken him back to the other side, but it would be the God of Elijah who did it. Elisha would have to discover God for himself, as we all must. We can go only so far with the God of our parents, pastors, and friends. Then Elisha picked up the mantle and struck the water saying, "Where is the Lord, the God of Elijah" (2 Kings 2:14). The water parted and he walked across. The sons of the prophets offered to search for his master, but Elisha refused. Because on the other side of the river, Elijah was his master, but on this side of the Jordan, God is his master.

God does not favor one of His children over another. All have been invited to His presence. We have our favorites, but God doesn't. It may appear that He favors one over another, but it only seems that way because some have chosen to draw near while others haven't. The blessing comes to those who hold on, who linger at the meetings, who go the extra mile to meet their Creator.

The Fourth Level of Intimacy

Finally, there is only one who continued on up the mountain of God. What was there about Moses that afforded such intimacy with God that He would speak to him face to face? Four issues stand out, and they constitute a challenge to all of us. The first is humility. It is recorded in Numbers 12:3, "Now the man Moses was very humble, more than any man who was on the face of the earth." I don't think that was the case from the beginning. Moses was raised in the courts of Pharaoh. This privileged position was orchestrated by God and would likely bring more pride than humility.

After rising to a strong political position of power, God placed a burden on his heart to set His people free. Did God put him in that high political position to accomplish that task? That would be a natural conclusion, but you don't set God's people free from any human position, political or otherwise. God works through our position in Christ to set captives free. Moses tried to accomplish God's work using his own strength and resources and failed and spent the next forty years tending his father-in-law's sheep on the far side of the desert.

Then one day this broken man turned aside to see a marvelous sight. A bush was burning, but not being consumed. He had been on fire once for God, but he burned out trying to serve God in his own strength and resources. He realized that the bush continued to burn on, because God was in the bush. God would set his people free, not Moses. He just wanted Moses to be the instrument He worked through, and the same follows for us. Pride is serving God in our own strength and resources. Humility is letting God work through us to accomplish His purposes.

Free from Selfish Ambition

Second, Moses was free from selfish ambition. After the people had built their own god, "The Lord said to Moses, 'I have seen this people, and behold, they are an obstinate people. Now then let me alone, that my anger may burn against them and that I may destroy them; and I will make of you a great nation" (Exodus 32:9,10). I wonder how many of us would pass that test. The people deserved judgment and God said he was going to carry it out and make a great nation of Moses. "Judge them, God. They deserve it, and by the way, great choice." So how did Moses respond (Ex. 32:11,12)?

> Then Moses entreated the Lord his God, and said, "O Lord, why does your anger burn against your people whom you have brought out from the land of Egypt with great power and with a mighty hand? Why should the Egyptians speak, saying. 'With evil intent, he brought them out to kill them in the mountains and to destroy them from the face of the earth'? Turn from your burning anger and change your mind about doing harm to your people.

Moses was more concerned about God's reputation than he was his own. He didn't want to build his own kingdom. He wanted to build God's kingdom. He wasn't trying to make a name for himself. Moses was proclaiming the great "I AM", who sent him back to Egypt to be an instrument in His hand. What name could we make for ourselves that would be more significant than being called children of God? What values rank higher than being eternally related to the One who "upholds all things by the word of his power" (Hebrews 1:3).

The Sabbath Rest

Third, Moses had the right goal. He had the formidable task of leading a couple of million grumbling Israelites across a barren land for forty years. There would be no running water, sinks, commodes, showers, bedrooms for privacy, or kitchens for cooking. They would have a one-course meal of manna, day after day after day. Babies would be conceived and delivered. Disputes would have to be settled and criticism deflected. Then Moses said to the Lord (Exodus 33:12-14):

> "See, you say to me, 'Bring up this people!' But you yourself have not let me know whom you will send with me. Moreover, you have said, 'I have known you by name, and you have also found favor in my sight.' Now then, if I have found favor in your sight in any way, please let me know your ways so that I may know you, in order that I may find favor in your sight. Consider too, that this nation is your people." And he said, "My presence shall go with you, and I will give you rest."

Trekking around the Sinai Peninsula for forty years is not my idea of rest, but God gave Moses rest. The quality of rest is measured by how you feel at the end. Forty years later Moses is standing on Mount Nebo looking into the Promised Land, which he never got to enter. "Although Moses was 120 years old when he died, his eyesight was not dim, nor had his vigor left him." (Deuteronomy 34:7). Resting in God is not an abdication of responsibility, nor the cessation of labor. Biblical rest is knowing God and His ways and living by faith in the power of the Holy Spirit.

Weariness comes from carrying our own load. Many stress-related illnesses that plague the world indicate an alienation from God and His ways. The writer of Hebrews says, "Consequently, there remains a Sabbath rest for the people of God." (4:9).

> Therefore, let us be diligent to enter that rest, so that no one will fall, through following the same example of disobedience. For the Word of God is living and active and sharper than any two-edged sword and piercing as far as the division of soul and spirit, of both joints and marrow, and able to judge the thoughts and intentions of the heart. And there is no creature hidden from his sight, but all things are open and laid bare to the eyes of him with whom we have to do.
>
> *Hebrews 4:11-13*

The "Word of God" mentioned above is not referring to the Bible. Jesus is the Word of God. The context clearly establishes that Jesus is the subject being discussed who is greater than the angels and greater than Moses. A book doesn't judge the thoughts and intentions of the heart. Jesus does. There is nothing hidden that won't be revealed. Secret sin on earth is open scandal in heaven.

A lady poured her heart out to me after a Sunday morning service. The self-disclosure ate away at her for the rest of the day. She called me Monday morning as soon as she thought it would be the right time and said, "I can't believe all the things I told you about myself yesterday. What do you think of me?" I said, "Well, I love you for sharing that with me. How else can I help you?" There was a pause and then she said, "Well I have a lot more to share with you then." Full disclosure happens naturally when doing so comes with acceptance and the hope of resolving past abuses and indiscretions.

Finally, Moses desired to see the glory of God. "Then Moses said, 'I pray you, show me your glory'" (Exodus 33: 18), and God did. Moses couldn't see God's face, but God's glory passed by, and Moses experienced the world's first afterglow. It transformed Moses, and his countenance radiated the glory of God, which slowly faded from his face. Such unusual encounters with God leave lasting impressions on our souls, but not necessarily our physical bodies, which are still destined to decay. Such encounters are not normative and may have a lasting physical impression such as with Saul who was blinded until he became Paul or a limp that stayed with Jacob when he became Israel.

I was studying in Israel and asleep in my hotel room when I was suddenly awakened by an overwhelming sense of God's presence. I saw and heard nothing, but I felt weightless and a taste of God's goodness. I was speechless, and all I kept saying in my mind was. "It's too good. Is this what it will be like in heaven? It's too good." It wasn't a dream. I woke the next morning with a clear memory of that experience. I will always remember it. It wasn't a game-changer at the time. I returned home and continued being a pastor and husband.

Many years later I realized the significance of that experience. God knew that I would have difficult days ahead. Twice, I took care of my ailing wife, and twice I lost everything I owned to pay medical expenses. My daughter was raped in her teenage years, and I have been publicly slandered. But never once did I question the goodness of God. I wasn't even tempted to think that way. Thank You, Jesus.

New Testament Intimacy with God

The Gospels also tell of the masses who came to see Jesus. Some came out of curiosity to see what all the fuss was about, and others for healing. Out of compassion, Jesus did heal the sick and then told some not to tell anyone. If the Lord's ministry was attested by signs and wonders, why would He say, "Don't tell anyone?" Because Jesus didn't come to heal the sick, restore sight and hearing to the blind and deaf, or to feed the 5,000. He knew the fickle nature of our fallen humanity. If He dealt only with their physical needs, that is all they would come to Him for, as people do today. Doing so may have shortened His public ministry which lasted only three years. If that be the case, then why did He do it? He did it because it was His nature to do it. "Seeing the people, He felt compassion for them" (Matthew 9:36). How wonderful it is for us to know that God is moved by compassion:

Matthew 14:14	for the multitude and the sick.
Matthew 15:32	for the hungry.
Matthew 18:27	for the enslaved.
Matthew 20:34	for the blind.
Mark 1:41	for the leper.
Mark 6:34	for those without a shepherd.
Luke 7:13	for those who grieve.
Luke 10:33	for the abused.
Luke 15:20	for the prodigals of this world.

Jesus said to those who questioned Him about dining with sinners, "But go and learn what this means: I desire compassion, and not sacrifice" (Matthew 9:13). We have become partakers of His divine nature (2 Peter 1:4), and those who are closest to Him will also be moved by compassion. Jesus cares about all our physical needs, but the real reason He came was to die for our sins on the cross and to be resurrected so that we could have new life in Christ. He reconciled us to God so that we may know Him and the power of His resurrection.

From the masses there were seventy that He chose to send out and proclaim the kingdom (Luke 10:1f). Then there were the twelve disciples who followed and assisted Jesus in His public ministry. Of the twelve, only Peter, James, and John went with Jesus up the mountain to pray (Luke 9:28) and witnessed the transfiguration. Finally, "There was reclining on Jesus' bosom one of his disciples, whom Jesus loved" (John 13:23). It was only John who went all the way to the cross. "When Jesus saw his mother, and the disciple whom he loved standing nearby, he said to his mother, 'Woman, behold, your son!' Then he said to the disciple, 'Behold, your mother!' From that hour the disciple took her into his own household" (John 19:26,27).

Jesus entrusted Mary to John who chose to go the final mile with God. There remains a vacant place upon the bosom of Jesus for all those who consider intimacy with God the most precious possession of all. He is the King of kings, the Lord of lords and the great I AM.

But to those of us who know Him personally, He is our Father, our Savior, our Lord, our Wonderful Counselor, our Great Physician, and our Friend.

As for me, I shall behold Your face in righteousness.

I will be satisfied with Your likeness when I awake.

Psalm 17:15

Discussion Questions

1. What is the difference between knowing God and knowing about God?
2. What two characteristics describe the least intimate with God?
3. What may happen to those on the second level of intimacy if they tire of waiting upon God, and haven't thought through the question, "So what if God exists?"
4. What was unique about Joshua?
5. What is the significance of crossing the Jordan?
6. How did Moses demonstrate his humility?
7. How did God test Moses to ensure that he was beyond selfish ambition and cared more about God's reputation than his own?
8. As we face difficult days ahead, what two questions should we be asking?
9. Since there is a coming apostasy before Christ's return, how can you ensure yourself that you will be like John and remain at the foot of the cross while others have deserted?
10. "Since all these things are to be destroyed in this way, what sort of people ought you to be in holy conduct and godliness" (2 Peter 3:11)?

Appendix A: Angels and Demons

The word "angel" means "messenger." The term primarily refers to heavenly beings, though it can mean a human messenger such as a prophet (see Haggai 1:13) or a priest (see Malachi 2:7). Other terms in the Bible refer to these angelic beings as "sons of God" (Genesis 6:2-4; Job 1:6, KJV); "heavenly beings" (Psalm 29:1); "holy ones" (Psalm 89:5); "heavenly host" (Luke 2:13); and "hosts," as in the phrase "LORD of hosts" (1 Samuel 1:11, KJV). The seraphim in Isaiah 6 also belong to the order of angels.

Angels are spiritual and majestic in nature. They existed before the creation of Adam and Eve, and their purpose is to execute God's will (see Psalm 148:2-5). They can pass from the spiritual realm to the physical realm at will, unimpeded by natural boundaries (see Acts 12:7). Angels also have superior intellect and wisdom (see 2 Samuel 14:17,20), but they are not omniscient (see Matthew 24:36). According to Jesus, they do not marry (see Luke 20:35-36). Psalm 103:20 summarizes the role and nature of angels: "Praise the LORD, you his angels, you mighty ones who do his bidding, who obey his word."

In the Bible, good angels consistently appear to people in human form on earth. They never appear as animals, reptiles, birds or material objects. There is no biblical record showing that a good angel ever appeared to wicked people or warned them of any danger. They are "ministering spirits sent to serve those who will inherit salvation" (Hebrews 1:14). Good angels always appeared to good people in human form as men. They never appeared as women or children, and they were always clothed. Just as Christ appeared in human form, so angels identified with humans in form, in speech, and in deed.

Sometimes the angels in the Bible were disguised so well as men that the people did not at first recognize them as angels. Abraham entertained "three men" as dinner guests. One remained to talk while the other two left to spend the night with Lot, who thought they were men (see Genesis 18:2; 19:1). Joshua did not know that the man standing before him was God's angel (see Joshua 5:13). Neither did Gideon realize that his guest was an angel until the angel made an offering of his meal (see Judges 6:21-22).

Occasionally, angels displayed themselves with a heavenly countenance and clothing that revealed the glory of God. In Luke 24:4, while the two women were lingering at the empty tomb of Jesus, "suddenly two men in clothes that gleamed like lightning stood beside them." In Daniel 10:5-6, the prophet gave a colorful description of an angel, "I lifted my eyes and looked, and behold, there was a certain man dressed in linen, whose waist was girded with a belt of pure gold of Uphaz. His body was like beryl, his face had the appearance of lightning, his eyes were like flaming torches, his arms and feet like the gleam of polished bronze, and the sound of his words like the sound of a tumult." On numerous occasions, angels were also described as "a man," or at least of having the appearance of a man (Ezekiel 40:3; Daniel 10:18; Zechariah 2:1).

Peter warns the Church about false teachers "who follow the corrupt desire of the flesh and despise authority. Bold and arrogant, they are not afraid to heap abuse on celestial beings; yet even angels, although they are stronger and more powerful, do not heap abuse on such beings when bringing judgment on them from the Lord" (2 Peter 2:10-11). Such restraint only reveals the angels' godly character, which stands in stark contrast to fallen humanity.

The Nature of Angels

In the original creation, all angels were good. However, when Satan led a rebellion against God, he took a third of the angels with him (Revelation 12:7-9). Now God commands His good angels and Satan commands a hoard of bad angels, who are identified as evil spirits or demons.

Contrary to the good angels, demons never appear in human form. People do see demonic apparitions or ghost-like appearances, but it is not "flesh and blood" (Ephesians 6:12). They are spirits who serve the evil desires of Satan. Satan functions as the ruler of this world through a demonic hierarchy. He is not omnipresent, so he reigns over his kingdom of darkness through rulers, authorities, powers of this dark world and "the spiritual forces of evil in the heavenly realms" (Ephesians 6:12).

In contrast to the evil nature of demons, good angels are called "the holy angels" (Luke 9:26), "the angels of God" (Luke 12:8), and "God's angels" (Hebrews 1:6). Jesus spoke of "His angels" (Matthew 16:27) and "angels in heaven" (Matthew 22:30). Paul referred to God's "powerful angels" (2 Thessalonians 1:7).

Of these good angels, only two in the Bible are mentioned by name. The first is Michael, whom Jude calls the archangel (see Jude 1:9). Michael disputed with Satan concerning the body of Moses and invoked the name of the Lord to rebuke him. In Daniel, Michael is called "one of the chief princes" (10:13). In Revelation, Michael is portrayed as the commander of the army of good angels who defeated and expelled the bad angels from heaven (12:7-8).

Gabriel is the other angel named in the Bible. He is the chief messenger angel who announced the births of John the Baptist and Jesus (see Luke 1:13,26-38). He interpreted Daniel's dream and delivered God's decree during the same mission (see Daniel 8:15-27).

"The angel of the Lord" seems to be a unique angel in the Old Testament. This angel announced the birth of Samson (see Judges 13:3-5) much like Gabriel did to Mary. When Manoah asked the angel of the Lord what his name was, he replied, "Why do you ask my name? It is beyond understanding'" (verse 18). The use of the definite article "the" in "the angel of the Lord" has led some to speculate that this may be a pre-incarnate appearance of Christ. The same speculation has been made about the "man" who wrestled with Jacob and told him that he had struggled with God (see Genesis 32:22-31).

Several conclusions can be drawn from the angelic visitation to Manoah. First, angels have a specific assignment from God, which they strictly follow. Manoah prayed that God would send the angel again to teach them how to raise the child, and the Lord granted a second visit, but the angel simply repeated his earlier message. Second, they communicate audibly in the same language and through the same medium that humans do. Third, they take on a physical form that can be seen by any person present. Fourth, they may not always be recognized as angelic beings, but they are recognized as men of God (see Judges 13:6,16). Fifth, they can change their form as they depart from our presence (see verse 20). All this stands in stark contrast to demons.

The Ministry of Angels

Angels are mediators of God's love and goodwill toward humankind, and their mission is always benevolent, which can be summarized in the following five ways.

First, angels announce and forewarn. An angel announced in advance to Abraham and Sarah the conception and birth of their son Isaac (see Genesis 18:9-14). The angel of the Lord foretold the birth of Samson (see Judges 13:2-24). Gabriel announced the birth of John the Baptist and Jesus (see Luke 1:13,30). An angel announced the birth of Jesus to the shepherds, and suddenly a chorus of heavenly hosts joined them in praising God. Angels also forewarned the righteous of imminent danger. An angel forewarned Abraham and Lot about the destruction of Sodom and Gomorrah (see Genesis 18:16–19:29). An angel also warned Joseph to flee to Egypt (see Matthew 2:13).

Second, angels guide and instruct. Abraham had repeated conversations with angels, and they guided him during his sojourn (see Genesis 24:7). When Moses led the Israelites out of Egypt, the angel of God guided them (see Exodus 14:19). During the Exodus, God told them, "See, I am sending an angel ahead of you to guard you along the way and to bring you to the place I have prepared" (23:20). An angel gave instructions to Cornelius (see Acts 10:3-7).

Third, angels guard and defend. "The angel of the LORD encamps around those who take refuge in him" (Psalm 34:7). An angel made Balaam revise his prophecy and rewrite his sermon (see Numbers 22:21-38). God's angelic army stood by to defend Elisha and his servant (see 2 Kings 6:17). An angel prevented Abraham from sacrificing Isaac (see Genesis 22:9-12) and protected the lives of Daniel and his three Hebrew friends (see Daniel 3:28; 6:22). The angel of death slew the firstborn of Egypt to force Pharaoh to release the Israelites (see Exodus 12:23). The angel of the Lord slew the army of Sennacherib to keep him from destroying Jerusalem (see 2 Kings 19:35). Jesus said He could have called on 12 legions of angels to save Himself (see Matthew 26:53).

John Patton, a missionary in New Hebrides, was once surrounded by hostile natives who were intent on burning down his mission headquarters. He and his wife were alone. They prayed for divine protection all night and were amazed the next morning to see the attackers leave for no apparent reason. A year later, the chief of the tribe converted to Christ, and John asked why he and his men had left that night. The chief replied in surprise, "Who were all those men you had there with you – hundreds of men in shining garments?"[38]

Fourth, angels minister to our needs. Peter was in great need when an angel released his chains and marched him out of prison (Acts 12:6-11). An angel ministered to Elijah when he was exhausted and fed him some hot cakes and water (see 1 Kings 19:5-7). After Jesus fasted for 40 days and was tempted by the devil, the "angels attended him" (Mark 1:13).

Fifth, angels assist in judgment. When the people shouted that Herod spoke as God, "Immediately, because Herod did not give praise to God, an angel of the Lord struck him down, and he was eaten by worms and died" (Acts 12:23). The sheep and the goats will be divided "when the Son of Man comes in his glory, and all the angels with him" (Matthew 25:31).

The Nature of Demons

After Jesus cast out a demon that had rendered a man mute, His detractors accused Him of casting out demons by the power of "Beelzebul, the prince of demons" (Luke 11:15). Jesus' following discussion about demons in verses 24-26 reveal a great deal about their nature and personality.

First, demons can exist inside or outside of humans. Demons have no physical means of expressing themselves except through human or animal agents. They seem to find a measure of rest in organic beings, even preferring swine to nothingness (see Mark 5:12). Evil spirits may assert territorial rights and be associated with certain geographical locations.

Second, demons are able to travel at will. Being spiritual entities, demons are not subject to the physical barriers of the natural world. The walls of church buildings do not provide a sanctuary, nor does our skin serve as a spiritual barrier. This is why we put on the armor of God. The only true sanctuary is our position in Christ.

Third, demons are able to communicate with each other. They can speak to humans through a human subject, as when they spoke to Christ through the Gadarene demoniac (see Matthew 8:28-34). We can also pay attention to deceiving spirits in our minds, which Paul warned us about: "But I am afraid that just as Eve was deceived by the serpent's cunning, your minds may somehow be led astray from your sincere and pure devotion to Christ" (2 Corinthians 11:3). People all over the world are struggling with condemning and blasphemous thoughts that are not of their choosing.

Fourth, every evil spirit has a separate identity. "When an impure spirit comes out of a person, it goes through arid places seeking rest and does not find it. Then it says, 'I will return to the house I left'" (Luke 11:24). Notice the use of personal pronouns. Demons are thinking personalities, not impersonal forces. Demons are like cockroaches. They operate under the cloak of darkness, and when the light is turned on, they scurry for the shadows. Their mission is always clandestine, and even their victims are not aware that they are being deceived.

Fifth, demons have the ability to remember and make plans. They can leave a person, remember the former state of the person, and come back with other demons. They obviously have the ability to think strategically.

Sixth, demons are able to evaluate and make decisions. The demons found "the house swept clean and put in order" (Luke 11:25). They can evaluate the condition of an intended victim and take advantage of a person's vulnerability.

Seventh, demons are able to combine forces. Notice in verse 26 that the one spirit joined with a group of seven other spirits, making the last state of the victim worse than before. In the case of the Gadarene demoniac, a number of them had united together—hence their name "Legion" (Mark 5:9).

Eighth, demons vary in degrees of wickedness. The first demon brought back seven others "more wicked than itself" (Luke 11:26). Jesus indicated degrees of wickedness and power when he said, "This kind can come out only by prayer" (Mark 9:29). These variations in power and wickedness fit the hierarchy described in Ephesians 6:12.

The Work of Demons

The Bible records extreme cases in which demons inhabited humans. In Mark 1:21-28, a demon spoke through a man in a synagogue. "'Be quiet!' said Jesus sternly. 'Come out of him!' The impure spirit shook the man violently and came out of him with a shriek" (verses 25-26). The Gadarene demoniac had many demons in him (see Mark 5:1-20). He exhibited supernatural strength by breaking the chains that bound him; no human was strong enough to subdue him. Somehow these demons were able to control the man's central nervous system, enabling them to speak through the man. When the evil spirits left, the man's rational capacities were restored.

Another man brought his son to Jesus saying, "A spirit seizes him, and he suddenly screams; it throws him into convulsions so that he foams at the mouth. It scarcely ever leaves him and is destroying him" (Luke 9:39). This was not a natural epileptic seizure. Jesus rebuked the evil spirit, healed the boy and gave him back to his father (see verse 42).

Likewise, a woman in a synagogue "had been crippled by a spirit for eighteen years. She was bent over and could not straighten up at all" (Luke 13:11). This was not osteoporosis. Jesus said Satan had kept her bound (see verse 16). More than 25 percent of those physically healed in the Gospel of Mark are the result of having been set free from demonic influences. Most physical illnesses come to us naturally, such as epilepsy and osteoporosis, but there may be another cause. We would have nothing to lose—but maybe much to gain—by verbally saying,

> "Lord, I submit my body to You as a living sacrifice, and I ask You to fill me with Your Holy Spirit. In the name and authority of the Lord Jesus Christ. I command Satan and all evil spirits to leave my presence."

The major spiritual work of demons is to tempt, accuse and deceive the minds of people. It is common for the secular world to diagnose certain individuals as being mentally ill when the real issue is the spiritual battle being waged for their minds. "The Spirit clearly says that in later times some will abandon the faith and follow deceiving spirits and things taught by demons" (1 Timothy 4:1). If we are deceived and believe a lie, it affects our mental and emotional health, which often shows up physically as a psychosomatic illness. Irenaeus wrote in the second century,

> "The devil, however, as he is the apostate angel, can only go to this length, as he did at the beginning, to deceive and lead astray the mind of man into disobeying the commandments of God, and gradually to darken the hearts[39]."

Appendix B: Freedom in Christ's Core Values

The Authority of Scripture (2 Timothy 3:16,17)

The basis for the message and methods of the ministry of Freedom in Christ Ministries (FICM) is the Word of God. The written Word and the Living Word should be seen as inseparable. Jesus is the Truth and so is His Word. FICM appreciates the contribution of empirical research and scientific investigation when the results are interpreted through the grid of Scripture. Science is mankind's attempt to understand natural law. Theology is the Christian's attempt to systematize divine revelation. Science and theology are fallible, but God's Word isn't. Freedom in Christ Ministries is committed to Truth and not any one particular systematic theology and does not see any incongruity between natural law and divine revelation, since both originate in God. All those under the spiritual authority of FICM are to be subject to God's Word and all governing authorities established by God (Romans 13:1-5).

The Centrality of Christ (Hebrews 12:1-3)

Our identity, acceptance, security, and significance are all found in Christ, who is the ultimate revelation of God. Therefore, our purpose is to help Christians, their marriages, and their ministries be established alive and free in Christ. God has given the Church, and consequently FICM, the ministry of reconciliation, which removes the barriers to having an intimate relationship with our Heavenly Father through repentance and faith in God.

Worshiping God and Praying (John 4:23)

Worship is to ascribe and embrace the true attributes of God, both corporately and individually, and then live accordingly. We strive to practice the presence of God and consider prayer our first priority, seeking to know Him and to do His will. We don't try to manipulate God or persuade Him to our point of view. We desire to be on the path that He has chosen for us, and choose to identify with Jesus when He said, "Not my will be done, but Your will be done." We try to bathe everything we do in prayer, not asking God to bless our plans, but submitting to His plans as discerned in prayer. We believe that Paul's instruction in Ephesians 6 on the armor of

God concludes with the admonition for all believers to pray at all times in the Spirit. The prayers that God the Holy Spirit prompts us to pray are the prayers that God answers. God uses such prayers to accomplish His work through us.

The Unity of Believers (John 17:20-23)

We serve the one true God who manifests Himself as the Father, Son, and Holy Spirit. The unity of the Godhead serves as the model for all relationships. We work to preserve the unity of the Spirit in the bond of peace (Ephesians 4:3). Where Satan works to divide our minds, marriages, and ministries, FICM works for the oneness of mind, marriage, and ministry as peacemakers (Matthew 5:9).

Our Identity in Christ (John 1:12)

Those who put their trust in Christ are children of God. They are no longer "in Adam," they are spiritually alive "in Christ." To be spiritually alive means that our souls are in union with God. Christians are new creations in Christ (2 Corinthians 5:17), and they are no longer "in the flesh," but they can walk after or according to the flesh (Romans 8:11). Those who are not yet Christians have neither the presence of God in their lives nor the knowledge of His ways, consequently their minds have been programmed to live independently of God. Salvation doesn't bring instant renewal of our minds, which is why the Apostle Paul warns us not to be conformed any longer to this world but to be transformed by the renewing of our minds (Romans 12:2). We believe that Scripture identifies all believers as saints rather than sinners, which does not necessarily reflect our maturity, just our position in Christ. All Christians are identified with Christ in His death (Romans 6:3; Galatians 2:20), in His burial (Romans 6:4), In His resurrection (Romans 6:5,8,11), In His ascension (Ephesians 2:6), In His life (Romans 5:10,11), In His power (Ephesians 1:19,20), and in His inheritance (Romans 8:16,17; Ephesians 1:11,12).

A Balanced Biblical Worldview (Ephesians 6:10-20)

We recognize the reality of the spiritual world and seek to be filled and guided by the Holy Spirit. We understand that the enemies of our sanctification are the world, the flesh, and the devil. There is a present spiritual battle between good and evil, between the kingdom of God and the kingdom of darkness, between the Spirit of truth, and the father of lies, and between the true prophets and the false prophets, which calls for Christians to have a solid biblical foundation, exercise discernment and keep their focus on Christ. We wrestle not with flesh and blood, but with spiritual rulers and authorities of this present darkness with the understanding that they have been disarmed (Colossians 2:15). We understand this battle to be more of a truth encounter rather than a power encounter, since the devil is already defeated.

A Holistic Answer to the Problems of Life (Matthew 6:19-34)

We try to avoid simplistic answers that address only one dimension of life and try to consider the proper functioning of our bodies, souls, and spirits. First, we teach the need for a balance of rest. exercise, and diet, and respect the role that medicine, and medications play in healing and maintaining the body. Second, we acknowledge psychosomatic illnesses, believe that emotional needs can be met in Christ, and seek to resolve the problems of fear, anxiety, panic attacks, depression, and addiction. Third, we consider the spiritual component of all problems, which includes the necessity of being connected to God and the need to escape from the devil's snares. We have a whole God, who deals with the whole of humanity and takes into account all reality, all the time, and we seek Him and His kingdom first.

Balancing God's Sovereignty and Mankind's Responsibility (1 Corinthians 3:4-9)

We cannot ask God to do for us what He has revealed to be our responsibility, and we cannot do for ourselves what only God can do. Any attempt by one person to help another should be done with the understanding that God is also present and there is a role that God and only God can play in each of our lives. Only God can set a captive free and bind up the broken-hearted person. So, we seek to establish our methods of ministry with the awareness of God's omnipresence, omniscience, and omnipotence. We also seek to understand the sensitive relationship that exists between the encourager and the inquirer, helping them to realize their responsibility. As reconcilers and encouragers, we also depend upon God and avoid being enablers, co-dependents, and rescuers, undermining the need for inquirers to be responsible for their attitudes and actions.

The Knowledge of God's Will (1 Thessalonians 4:3)

We believe that God will guide all those who seek to follow Him, which is a different concept than knowing God's will. God's will for our lives is our sanctification, i.e., we conform to His image. The goal of our instruction is love (1 Timothy 1:5), which is the character of God (1 John 4:16), and not knowledge that makes one arrogant (1 Corinthians 8:1). God is not trying to enlarge our minds; He is trying to enlarge our hearts so that we may be like Him. We can have knowledge and be arrogant, but we cannot know God and be arrogant. Our goal is to know God and become like Him (Philippians 3:8-14) so that others will know that we are servants of God, because of His love shining through us.

The Grace of God (2 Corinthians 3:5,6)

We believe that we are servants of a new covenant, for the law kills, but the Spirit gives life. Grace is neither legalism nor license. We could not live up to the law by the law, but we can live a righteous life if we do so by faith according to what God says is true and by doing so in His power rather than by our own strength and resources. Part of our purpose is to help Christians and their ministries to move from a works and program orientation to a grace and faith orientation. Biblical strategies and programs will not work unless they are empowered by the life of God, because apart from Christ we cannot do anything of lasting consequence (John 15:5). We don't have to bear fruit; we have to abide in Christ and then we will bear fruit. Ministering grace also means that we don't put a price tag on our ministry or charge a fee for freedom appointments.

Servant Leadership (Matthew 20:20-28)

We don't get our significance from titles, degrees, gifts, or ecclesiastical positions. We strive to be significant and secure in Christ, and not Lord it over others (1 Peter 5:1-11). The qualifications to be a spiritual leader (1 Timothy 3:1-13; Titus 1:6-9) are all related to Godly character. As servant leaders, we choose to walk in the light and speak the truth to one another in love. We want every Christian to reach their highest potential and use their talents and gifts to glorify God and edify others. It is the purpose of FICM to empower God's people by helping them to understand who they are in Christ, enabling them to be all that God intended them to be so they will be able to do all things through Christ who strengthens them (Philippians 4:13).

Integrity and Authenticity

Spiritual integrity and authenticity are more important than recognition, and perceived impact. We believe the proper order is to have maturity before ministry, character before career, and being before doing. Who we are is more important than what we do, and we should never compromise ourselves or our message in order gain the approval of others. God's work done God's way will never lack His support, therefore we don't subscribe to worldly methods of fundraising, exaggeration, hype, false pretenses, exploitation, and self-promotion. Our focus is to grow in our maturity, bring clarity, correctness, and balance to our message, and let God expand our ministry.

Freedom in Christ Resources

Can We Help You Make Fruitful Disciples?

A church with growing, fruitful disciples of Jesus is a growing, fruitful church that is making a real difference in the community where God has placed it. A key question for church leaders is: "How can I help our people become mature, fruitful disciples as quickly as possible so that they go out and make a real impact?"

A fundamental part of the answer is to help them understand the principles that underlie all of Freedom in Christ's discipleship resources for churches:

- TRUTH - Know who you are in Christ.
- TURNING - Ruthlessly close any doors you've opened to the enemy through past sin and don't open any more
- TRANSFORMATION - Renew your mind to the truth of God's Word (which is how you will be transformed).

Freedom In Christ has equipped hundreds of thousands of church leaders around the world to use this "identity-based discipleship" approach. As churches base their discipleship around these principles, they report not only changed individual lives but whole changed churches. When churches start to look less like hospitals, full of those who are constantly struggling with their own issues and more like part of the Bride of Christ, they make an increasing impact on their community.

Our mission is to equip the Church to transform the nations by providing church leaders with transformational discipleship resources that can be used right across their church. Some are specially tailored to the communication styles of different groups such as young people and millennials. Others build on our main Freedom in Christ Course. You can see some of them on the following pages.

Our heart is to help church leaders develop a long-term, whole-church discipleship strategy. Our offices and representatives around the world run training courses and have people on the ground who like nothing better than to discuss discipleship with church leaders. If you think we can help you in any way as you look to make fruitful disciples, please get in touch.

Find your local office at: FreedomInChrist.org.

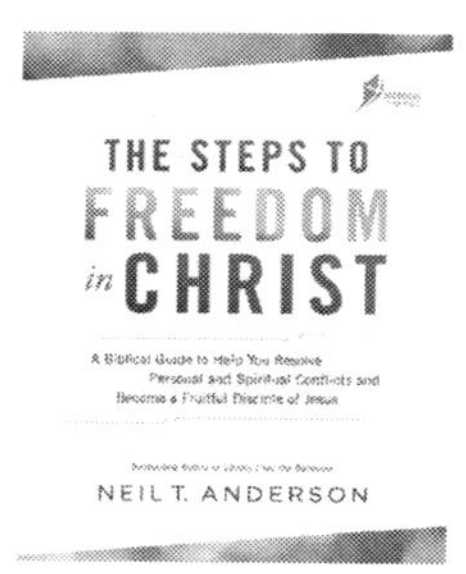

Take Hold of The Freedom That Is Yours in Christ!

- Do you want to become an even more fruitful disciple of Jesus?
- Are you tired of not fulfilling your full potential as a Christian?

All Christians need to come to know and understand their identity, position, and authority in Christ. Knowing those truths helps a believer in Jesus become a growing, fruitful disciple (follower) of Christ. God has greatly gifted Dr. Neil T. Anderson to present the biblical truths of our identity and freedom in Christ in a wonderful God-directed, liberating way. These truths are described in the books *Victory Over the Darkness*, and *The Bondage Breaker* which became the foundation of Freedom in Christ Ministries. But this teaching did not originate with Dr. Anderson, it is straight from the New Testament and is new covenant Christianity brought to us initially by the apostles Paul, Peter, and John and further developed by the early Church fathers.

The Steps to Freedom in Christ is a biblically-based ministry tool that is derived from James 4:7— "Submit to God, resist the devil and he will flee from you." It is a gentle process of following the Holy Spirit's prompting to deal with the effects of any sin committed by you or against you.

Going through *The Steps to Freedom in Christ* is taking personal responsibility for your life and spiritual growth. It is a systematic approach of examining your heart and life before the Lord and asking Him to reveal areas of your life where there are unresolved sin issues in the light of Scripture. Accordingly, you choose to confess, repent and renounce whatever is standing between you and your spiritual freedom, identify lies believed, and replace them with God's truth.

The Freedom in Christ Course

Now in its third edition and translated into well over 30 languages, The Freedom in Christ Course can transform the way you help Christians become fruitful disciples. Focused on first establishing every Christian in the sure foundation of their identity in Jesus, it gives them the tools to break free and stay free from all that holds them back, and a strategy for ongoing transformation. It has ten teaching sessions presented by Steve Goss, Nancy Maldonado, and Daryl Fitzgerald plus *The Steps to Freedom in Christ* ministry component presented by Steve Goss and Neil Anderson.

With a specially designed app, extra teaching films, a worship album, a Leader's Guide, a Participant's Guide, and tons of extras, The Freedom in Christ Course offers you everything you need to make disciples who bear fruit that will last!

"Men, women, and middle and high school students have been radically transformed."
Bob Huisman, Pastor, Immanuel Christian Reformed Church
Hudsonville, MI, USA

"I recommend it highly to anyone serious about discipleship."
Chuah Seong Peng, Senior Pastor, Holy Light Presbyterian Church
Johor Baru, Malaysia

"*The Freedom in Christ Course* changed me and put me in a position to minister to people in a much more effective way."
Frikkie Elstadt, Every Nation Patria
Mossel Bay, South Africa

"Our church has changed as a result of this course. Those who come to Christ and who do the course end up with a rock-solid start to their faith."
Pastor Sam Scott, Eltham Baptist Church
Australia

The Grace Course

If you don't first know God's love for you in your heart – not just your head – it's impossible for your life to be motivated by love for Him. Instead, you are likely to end up motivated more by guilt or shame or fear or pride. You may be doing all the "right" things, believing all the right things and saying all the right things, but there will be precious little fruit.

- Six sessions plus *The Steps to Experiencing God's Grace*.

Present it yourself or use the video presentations.
Video testimonies illustrating the teaching points, practical exercises, times of listening to God, and Pause for Thought times.
Works especially well as a course during Lent.

"For the first time in the decades that I've been a Christian, I'm suddenly 'getting' grace – it's amazing and it's shocking!"

"I realized that it's not about my performance – He just wants my heart."

"It was AMAZING! During the last session, after we had finished nobody moved for what seemed like ages. When the silence eventually did break, people began to share all that the course had meant to them spontaneously. Testimonies to what the Lord had done just flowed out, some were life changing."

"*The Grace Course* does a marvelous job of introducing the concept of grace in a simple, engaging and, at times, even humorous way. It is short and to the point, taking an incredibly deep theological issue and making it understandable and practical."

Disciple – FICM's Message for The Millennial Generation

Church leaders report that discipling those in their 20s and 30s is one of their biggest challenges. disciple is a powerful tool to help you. It speaks the language of 20s and 30s and invites them to dive into the greatest story ever told God's story. They will learn how to take hold of their freedom and discover their mandate.

Ten sessions designed to run for approximately 90 minutes each.

- Impactful Starter Films introduce the theme for each session.
- Extra films (via the app) on topics including sex, the occult, and fear.
- Chat and Reflect times allow teaching to take root.
- App with extra teaching films, daily devotional, daily nuggets of extra teaching, and *Stronghold–Buster-Builder* with reminders.

"Thank you so much for caring enough to do this. You have no idea how much it means to us that you have taken the time to understand and help us overcome all the stuff that comes at us."

"You really get us and understand us, you don't patronize us and talk down to us."

"God is doing incredible things in the young people at our church and I'm just grateful this course has been able to facilitate that."

"*Disciple* is really user-friendly. The young adults really engaged and there were definite light bulb moments."

Freed to Lead

Freed To Lead is a ten-week discipleship course for Christians who are called to leadership – whether in the marketplace, public service, the Church or any other context. It will transform your leadership, free you from drivenness and burnout, enable you to survive personal attacks, use conflict positively, and overcome other barriers to effective leadership.

- Ten sessions plus *The Steps to Freedom for Leaders*.
- Video testimonies and Pause for Thought discussion times.
- Ideal for church leadership teams before rolling out across the church.

"The Freed to Lead course has been the most amazing leadership development experience of my career, having been called to both marketplace and church leadership for over twenty years. It dispels worldly leadership myths and practices and provides Biblical foundations for Godly leadership. I wholeheartedly recommend this course for anyone who aspires or is currently called to Godly servant-hearted leadership in any arena."

"An outstanding course – inspirational and motivational, affirming and encouraging."

"It has reinforced my conviction that my identity is first and foremost in Christ, whatever leadership role I may hold."

The Lightbringers for Children

The Lightbringers is a powerful resource for churches and parents to use with 5-to-11-year-olds. It is designed to equip them to become fruitful disciples who stay connected to Jesus into their adu t lives. They w ll understand:

- Who they are in Jesus.
- What they have in Jesus.
- How to become fruitful disciples who follow Jesus closely.

It consists of ten action-packed sessions plus specially written versions of *The Steps to Freedom in Christ* ministry component and has versions for two age groups (5-8 and 9-11). It's great for churches, Bible clubs, and families.

The Church Edition includes a comprehensive 276-page Leader's Guide, downloadable videos, songs, activity sheets, and PowerPoint presentations. The Family Edition is an online-only version designed to be delivered in the home.

"Parents, educators, children's leaders, and pastors rejoice! There is no longer a void in quality children's curriculum that instills the essentials of identity in Christ and freedom in Christ."

"The Lightbringers is a fantastic resource to help children know their identity in Christ and how to view the rest of the world through that lens."

"It has awesome content, is easy to follow, and wi l fill what has been a huge gap in kids' ministry up to this time."

On-Demand Videos for Our Courses

You can access all of our video material for small group studies online for one low monthly subscription. Try it for free!

Access to all the main Freedom in Christ small group courses so you can browse or use the entire range including:

- *The Freedom in Christ Course*
- *The Lightbringers – Freedom in Christ for Children*
- *Freedom In Christ for Young People*
- *Disciple* (the Freedom in Christ message for ages 18 to 30s)
- *The Grace Course*
- *Freed To Lead*
- *Keys To Health, Wholeness, & Fruitfulness*

Free video training courses for course leaders and their teams:

- *Making Fruitful Disciples* – the Biblical principles of discipleship
- *Helping Others Find Freedom in Christ*

No need to buy several DVD sets if you have multiple groups running. Access is for all members of your church so participants can catch up if they miss a session.

For further information, pricing, and to start your free trial go to:

FreedomInChrist.org/FreedomStream

Get in Touch.

Freedom In Christ exists to equip the Church to make fruitful disciples who make a real impact in their community. Our passion is to help church leaders develop a discipleship strategy right across their church that will be effective for years to come. How can we help your church?

We offer:

- A series of introductory and training events for church leaders.
- Advice on establishing a discipleship strategy for your church built around our discipleship resources.
- Training and equipping for those in your church who will be involved in implementing that strategy.

For contact details of Freedom in Christ in your country or to find out how to order our resources, go to:

FreedomInChrist.org

Freedom in Christ Ministries Books and Resources

Core Material

Victory Over the Darkness has a companion study guide, DVD, and an audiobook edition (Bethany House, 2000). With more than 1,400,000 copies in print, this core book explains who you are in Christ, how to walk by faith in the power of the Holy Spirit, how to be transformed by the renewing of your mind, how to experience emotional freedom, and how to relate to one another in Christ.

The Bondage Breaker has a companion study guide, and audiobook edition (Harvest House Publishers, 2000). With more than 1,400,000 copies in print, this book explains spiritual warfare, our protection, how we are vulnerable, and how we can live a liberated life in Christ.

The Steps to Freedom in Christ and the companion interactive video (SPCK / Bethany House, 2017) are discipleship counseling tools that help Christians resolve their personal and spiritual conflicts through genuine repentance and faith in God.

Discipleship Counseling (Bethany House, 2003) combines the concepts of discipleship and counseling and teaches the practical integration of theology and psychology helping Christians resolve their personal and spiritual conflicts through genuine repentance and faith in God.

Restored is an expansion of *The Steps to Freedom in Christ* with additional explanation and instruction. It can be freely downloaded at www.restored.pub.

Walking In Freedom (Bethany House, 2009) is a 21-day devotional to be used for follow-up after processing *The Steps to Freedom in Christ.*

"Victory Series" (Bethany House, 2014 - 2015) is a comprehensive curriculum, including eight books that follow the growth sequence of being rooted in Christ, growing in Christ, living in Christ, and overcoming in Christ: *God's Story for You; Your New Identity; Your Foundation in Christ; Renewing Your Mind; Growing in Christ; Your Life in Christ; Your Authority in Christ; Your Ultimate Victory.*

Other Discipleship Courses

Keys To Health, Wholeness & Fruitfulness Bringing together the truth from the Bible and wisdom from the medical world, the course will equip you to be a healthy, whole disciple of Jesus whose life really counts.

Specialized Books

The Bondage Breaker, The Next Step (Harvest House, 2011) includes several testimonies of people who found their freedom from all kinds of problems, with commentary by Dr. Anderson. It is an important learning tool for encouragers and gives hope to those who are entangled in sin.

Overcoming Addictive Behavior with Mike Quarles (Bethany House, 2003) explores the path to addiction and how a Christian can overcome addictive behaviors.

Overcoming Depression with Joanne Anderson (Bethany House, 2004) explores the nature of depression, which is a body, soul, and spirit problem and presents a wholistic answer for overcoming this "common cold" of mental illnesses.

Daily in Christ with Joanne Anderson (Harvest House, 2000) is a popular daily devotional read by thousands of internet subscribers every day.

Who I Am in Christ (Bethany House, 2001) has 36 short chapters describing who believers are in Christ and how their deepest needs are met in Him.

Freedom from Addiction with Mike and Julia Quarles (Bethany House, 1996) begins with Mike and Julia's journey into addiction and codependency and explains the nature of chemical addictions and how to overcome them in Christ.

One Day at a Time with Mike and Julia Quarles (Bethany House, 2000) is a 120-day devotional helping those who struggle with addictive behaviors and explaining how to discover the grace of God on a daily basis.

Letting Go of Fear with Rich Miller (Harvest House Publishers, 2018) explains the nature of fear, anxiety and panic attacks and how to overcome them.

Setting Your Church Free with Charles Mylander (Bethany House, 2014) explains servant leadership and how the leadership of a church can resolve corporate conflicts through corporate repentance.

Setting Your Marriage Free with Charles Mylander (Bethany House, 2014) explains God's divine plan for marriage and the steps that couples can take to resolve their difficulties.

Christ-Centered Therapy with Terry and Julianne Zuehlke (Zondervan, 2000) explains the practical integration of theology and psychology for professional counselors and provides them with biblical tools for therapy.

Managing Your Anger with Rich Miller (Harvest House, 2018) explains the nature of anger and how to put away all anger, wrath, and malice.

Grace That Breaks the Chains with Rich Miller and Paul Travis (Harvest House, 2014) explains the bondage of legalism and how to overcome it by the grace of God.

Winning the Battle Within (Harvest House, 2008) shares God's standards for sexual conduct, the path to sexual addiction and how to overcome sexual strongholds.

Restoring Broken Relationships (Bethany House, 2015) explains the church's primary ministry, and how we can be reconciled to God and each other.

Rough Road to Freedom (Monarch Books, 2012) is Dr. Anderson's memoir.

The Power of Presence (Monarch Books, 2016) is about experiencing the presence of God during difficult times and what our presence means to each other. This book is written in the context of Dr. Anderson caring for his wife, who was slowly dying of agitated dementia.

Endnotes

1   Ed Vitagliano, "The Decay of Greatness," AFA Journal, June 2011, 35:6, pp. 10-12

2   Ancient Christian Commentary, IVP, Downers Grove, Il. 2000, VIII, p. 121

3   Jesus quoted this passage when the Jews charged Him with blasphemy for claiming to be God. Jesus countered by saying, "Has it not been written in your Law, 'I said, you are gods'? If he called them gods, to whom the word of God came (and Scripture cannot be broken), do you say of Him, whom the Father sanctified and sent into the world, 'You are blaspheming,' because I said, 'I am the Son of God'?" (John 10:34-36).

4   Clinton E. Arnold, Powers of Darkness (Inter Varsity Press: Downers Grove, Ill. 1992)

5   Ancient Christian Commentary, IVP, Downers Grove, Il. 2000, VII, p. 22.

6   IBID

7   F.F. Bruce, Commentary on the Book of Acts (Grand Rapids, MI: Eerdmans, 1954), 114.

8   Ernst Haenchen, The Acts of the Apostles (Philadelphia: Westminster Press, 1971), 237.

9   Ancient Christian Commentary, IVP, Downers Grove, Il. 2000, VIII, p. 40,41.

10   Anderson, Miller, and Travis, Grace That Breaks the Chains, (Harvest House, Eugene, Oregon), 2003.

11   Clinton Arnold, Power of Darkness, (IVP, Downers Grove, Illinois, 1992) p. 54.

12   Neil T. Anderson, The Steps to Freedom in Christ, (Bethany House Publishers, Bloomington, Minnesota, 2017).

13   The Steps are explained in detail in my book Discipleship Counseling, published by Bethany House Publishers. They are also included and explained in my book Restored, which can be freely downloaded at www.restored.pub.

14   The "Living Free in Christ" conference, which I have taught around the world, is now our basic discipleship course entitled "Freedom in Christ," published by Bethany House Publishers, and is now available in many languages.

15   Ancient Christian Commentary, IVP, Downers Grove, Il. 2000, p. 290.

16   IBID

17   David W. Bercot, Editor, A Dictionary of Early Christian Beliefs, Hendrickson Publishers, Peabody, Massachusetts, 1998, p. 540.

18   IBID.

19   David W. Bercot, Editor, A Dictionary of Early Christian Beliefs, Hendrickson Publishers, Peabody, Massachusetts, 1998, p. 540.

20   Ancient Christian Commentary on Scripture, IVP, Downers Grove, Il. 2000, pp. 181,182.

21   Neil T. Anderson and Steve Russo, The Seduction of Our Children, (Harvest House Publishers, Eugene, OR, 1991), p. 33.

22   Martin Wells Knapp, Impressions (Wheaton, IL: Tyndale House Publishers, 1984), p. 32.

23   IBID, p. 43

24   IBID, p. 14

25   Neil T. Anderson & Charles Mylander, Setting Your Church Free, (Bethany House Publishers, Bloomington, Minnesota, 2006)

26   David W. Bercot, Editor, A Dictionary of Early Christian Beliefs, Hendrickson Publishers, Peabody, Massachusetts, 1998, p. 592.

27   IBID, p. 594.

28   For further information see An Introduction to Dissociative Identity Disorder, Bramhall & Goss, Freedom in Christ Ministries International, 2023

29   Ancient Christian Commentary on Scriptures, New Testament X, IVP, Downers Grove, IL., 2005, p. 79.

30   Ancient Christian Commentary on Scripture, IVP, Downers Grove, Il. 2000, pp. 24-26.

31   A.T. Robertson, Word Pictures in the New Testament (Grand Rapids, Baker Book House, 1930), p.134.

32   Ancient Christian Commentary on Scripture, New Testament VIII (IVP, Downers Grove, 1999), p. 202.

33   A. B. Simpson, The Life of Prayer and the Power of Stillness (Seattle: CreateSpace, 2010), pp.102-4

34   Ancient Christian Commentary on Scripture, New Testament VIII, (IVP, Downers Grove, IL., 1999) p. 82.

35   Walter Marshall, The Gospel-Mystery of Sanctification, (Zondervan, Grand Rapids, MI, 1954), p. 156.

36   David W. Bercot, Editor, A Dictionary of Early Christian Beliefs, (Hendrickson Publishers, Peabody, Mass. 2000) p.312.

37   https://westminstershortercatechism.net/god'saspirit/

38   Billy Graham, Angels: God's Secret Agents (Waco, TX: Word Books, 1986), p. 3.

39   St. Irenaeus, Against Heresies, Book 5, Chap. 24, c. AD 180

Made in the USA
Middletown, DE
29 September 2025